AMERICA'S
Patriotic Places

© Brigitta L. House/MICHELIN

5★0
Revered Sites

★ ★ ★ ★ ★ ★ ★ ★ ★

i

Chief Editor	Cynthia Clayton Ochterbeck
Senior Editors	Gwen Cannon, M. Linda Lee
Production Coordinator	Allison M. Simpson
Cartography	Peter Wrenn
Photo Editors	Allison M. Simpson
	Brigitta L. House
Documentation	Douglas Rogers
Design	Octavo Design, Apopka FL
Printing and Binding	Banta Book Group, Menasha WI

Contact us:
Michelin Travel Publications
One Parkway South
Greenville, SC 29615
Phone: 1-800-423-0485
www.michelin-us.com
email: TheGreenGuide-us@us.michelin.com

Cover Photo Credits:
Front: (*listed clockwise*)
The Liberty Bell ©Comstock.com; The Statue of Liberty ©Jeff Greenberg/ NYC & Company;
Marine Corps War Memorial ©PhotoDisc; Mount Rushmore ©Comstock.com.

Back: Washington Monument ©Washington D.C. Convention & Tourism Corporation

Note to the reader:
While every effort is made to ensure that all information in this publication is correct and up-to-date, Michelin Travel Publications (Michelin North America, Inc.) accepts no liability for any direct, indirect or consequential losses howsoever caused so far as such can be excluded by law.

"...One nation,

under God,

indivisible,

with liberty

and justice

for all."

★ ★ ★ ★ ★ ★ ★ ★

The 50 Patriotic Places and Their Locations

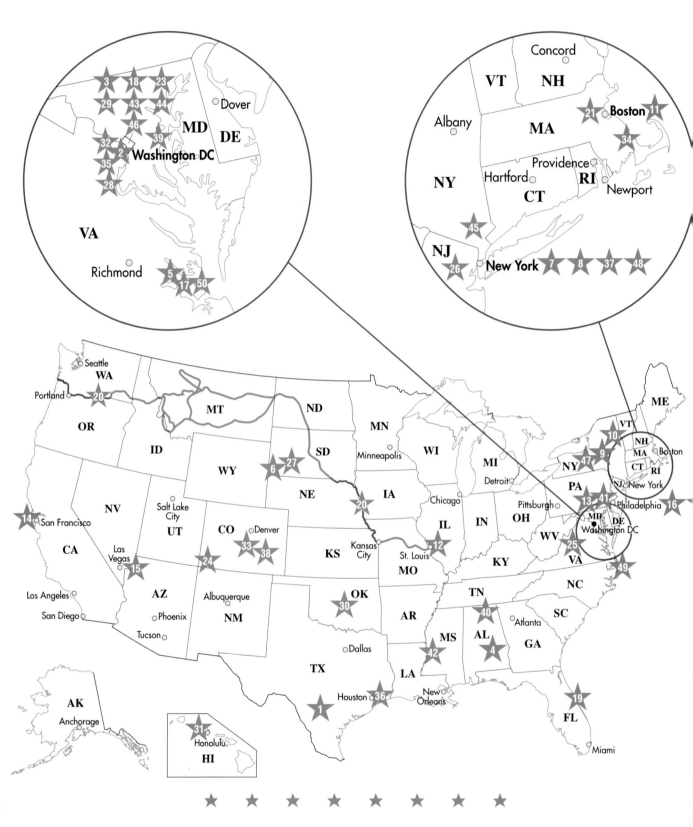

Table of Contents

(Listed Alphabetically)

★ ★ ★ ★ ★ ★ ★ ★

★ ★ ★ ★ ★ ★ ★ ★

Cradle of Texas Liberty
The Alamo

The Alamo — San Antonio CVB/Nancy H. Belcher

San Antonio, Texas

Popularly known as The Alamo, which means "cottonwood" in Spanish, Mission San Antonio de Valero is a timeless Texas icon. It stands as a tribute to courage in the face of overwhelming odds. "Remember the Alamo!" became the battle cry of the war for Texan independence. Built in 1718 by Franciscans and eventually abandoned, it served as a Spanish, then Mexican military post in the early 1800s before becoming the scene of a legendary "defend-to-the death" fight.

Defining Moments: 1836

Texas' struggle for independence from Mexico was in its early stages in December 1835, when rebels forced Mexican troops out of San Antonio and set up a stronghold inside The Alamo. Two months later Mexican president General Santa Anna and his army attacked the mission. For 13 days (February 23 to March 6, 1836), the 189 defenders held out against 4,000 soldiers until every rebel was killed. Among those who lost their lives were the celebrated Davy Crockett, renowned knife-fighter Jim Bowie, and commander William B. Travis.

"Remember the Alamo!"

Their heroic efforts served as an inspiration to others fighting for Texan independence. One month later, General Sam Houston and his small army defeated Santa Anna at San Jacinto, near the present-day city of Houston. When the Republic of Texas (1836–1845) was formed, Sam Houston was elected its president.

Key Figures
★★★★★★★
Sam Houston	(1793–1863)
Davy Crockett	(1786–1836)
Jim Bowie	(1796–1836)

   Restored and open to visitors, The Alamo is besieged these days by downtown traffic and even tourist traps, but the complex sits within a quiet courtyard. Exhibits inside focus on the historic event before and after the assault.

San Antonio

One of the most attractive cities in Texas, San Antonio was first the territory of Coahuiltecan Indians, then Spain, followed by France, Spain again and finally Mexico. After the Civil War, the town attracted cattle ranchers. Following severe flooding in 1921, the San Antonio River was converted to a covered storm sewer. In 1939 city officials began to change the eyesore into a tourist attraction, now the pleasant riverside shopping and dining promenade, which made its debut at the city's Hemis Fair 1968 world's fair.

San Antonio Riverwalk — © San Antonio CVB/Al Rendon

Address: 300 Alamo Plaza at Crockett Street

Phone: 210-225-1391

www.TheAlamo.org

Revered Burial Grounds
Arlington National Cemetery

Arlington, Virginia

The country's most recognized cemetery faces the Mall in Washington, D.C., just across the Potomac River, in Arlington. Lined with row after row of white headstones, this vast military cemetery holds the graves of many distinguished Americans.

Defining Moments: 1864

Early in the Civil War, Robert E. Lee's home, Arlington House, was occupied by Union forces and made headquarters for the defense of the nation's capital. Some 200 acres of his estate were set aside as a burial ground for war casualties. On May 13, 1864, the first soldier was laid to rest at the site. By 1883 the remains of 16,000 war victims had been interred here, and in that same year, Arlington became the official national cemetery of the United States.

A National Shrine

Today the cemetery's 612 acres contain the graves of more than 260,000 military personnel and their dependents. Veterans of every U.S.-involved armed conflict since the

Revolutionary War are buried here. The graves of presidents William H. Taft (1857–1930) and John F. Kennedy (1917–1963) are in Arlington Cemetery. The Tomb of the Unknowns contains the remains of soldiers who symbolize the lives of all men and women lost in combat.

Who Can Be Buried Here

Service personnel eligible for interment at Arlington include those who:

★ died on active duty;

★ were veterans retired from active duty or reserve service;

★ were honorably discharged for disability before October 1, 1949; or

★ held the country's highest military decorations (Medal of Honor, Silver Star, Purple Heart).

Other notable individuals laid to rest here are Claire Chennault, commander of the Flying Tigers in World War II; heavyweight boxing champion Joe Louis; Apollo I astronauts Virgil Grissom and Roger Chaffee; Supreme Court justice Oliver Wendell Holmes, Jr.; polar explorer Richard Byrd; inventor George Westinghouse; novelist Dashiell Hammett; and civil rights leader Medgar Evers.

A number of memorials have been placed in Arlington Cemetery: among them are those dedicated to the United Spanish War Veterans; the 101st Army Airborne Division; Women in Military Service for America; the Shuttle Challenger astronauts; service personnel killed in the attempt to rescue U.S. hostages in Iran, 1980; the U.S. Coast Guard; and victims of the crash of Pan Am Flight 103 over Lockerbie, Scotland. There's also a Rough Riders Memorial and a Confederate Monument. The cemetery's most prominent memorial, Arlington House, occupies a hilltop site overlooking the cemetery.

Address: Arlington side of Memorial Bridge

Phone: 703-697-2131

www.arlingtoncemetery.org

The Capitol Dome — © Washington, DC Convention and Tourism Corporation

Washington, D.C.

Center of the nation's government, the massive Capitol building anchors the eastern end of the capital city's Mall, the grassy, museum-lined avenue that extends to the Potomac River. A tiered, cast-iron, 180-foot-high dome rises above the building, crowned by a bronze statue of Freedom. One of the city's most prominent landmarks, this solid symbol of democracy-in-action has housed the Congress of the United States since 1800.

*"Who are the Congress?
Are they not the Creatures of the People?"*

George Washington, Letter to Reverend William Gordon, July 8, 1783

Defining Moments: 1793

The Capitol Building — © Brigitta L. House/MICHELIN

In the late 18th century, the first U.S. president, George Washington, and his secretary of State, Thomas Jefferson, held a public competition for designs for a capitol building. William Thornton, a respected amateur architect, won $500 and a city lot for his plan, which was modeled on the ancient Pantheon in Rome. On September 18, 1793, Washington oversaw the ceremonial laying of the building's cornerstone. The nation's second president, John Adams, addressed the first joint session of Congress in the completed north wing (the original Senate wing) seven years later. British architect Benjamin Henry Latrobe finished the south wing (the original House wing) by 1807.

During the War of 1812, the British set fire to the Capitol, gutting the interior. Working to restore it, Latrobe added domes over the two original wings and redesigned the House chamber (now Statuary Hall) in the semicircular shape it bears today. Boston architect Charles Bulfinch later served as the official architect of the Capitol, completing the building pretty much according to Thornton's original plans.

In 1850 Senator Jefferson Davis, who was to become president of the Confederacy, encouraged Congress to fund two new wings to house the growing Senate and House. Thomas U. Walter from Philadelphia was asked to draw up plans. Construction began in a climate of civil strife. During the Civil War, when Congress was not in session, the "Big Tent," as soldiers called the Capitol, housed troops and later served as a hospital for the wounded. Through all this, construction proceeded, as "a sign," President Lincoln declared, "that we intend the Union shall go on."

By the late 1950s Congress had once again outgrown the Capitol. To provide more space, the east facade was extended by just over 32 feet, giving it the appearance it has today.

Address: 1st Street N.W., between Independence and Constitution Avenue

Phone: 202-225-6827

www.aoc.gov

Struggle for Equality
Civil Rights Memorial

Montgomery, Alabama

The capital of Alabama serves as the setting for a stirring memorial to those killed between 1954 and 1968 in the struggle for civil rights. Outside the Southern Poverty Law Center, water flows ceaselessly over the names of 40 civil rights martyrs engraved on designer Maya Lin's round, table-like monument. Dated April 4, 1968 (the day he died), the last entry is the name of Baptist minister Dr. Martin Luther King, Jr., who, like the others, lost his life in the fight for justice and racial equality.

Civil Rights Memorial — © Alabama Bureau of Tourism & Travel/ Shams Basha

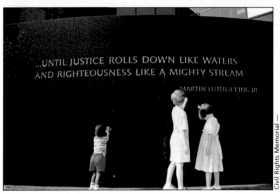

...UNTIL JUSTICE ROLLS DOWN LIKE WATERS AND RIGHTEOUSNESS LIKE A MIGHTY STREAM

MARTIN LUTHER KING JR.

Civil Rights Memorial — © Alabama Bureau of Tourism & Travel/ Dan Brothers

Defining Moments: 1955

Rosa Parks Statue — © Alabama Bureau of Tourism & Travel/ Karim Shamsi Basha

On December 1, 1955, black seamstress Rosa Parks boarded the bus she took home every night and took a seat. After she refused to move to the back so that a white passenger could sit in her place, she was arrested. Parks' arrest prompted the Montgomery bus boycott, when black citizens refused, for over a year, to take segregated buses, until the Supreme Court outlawed the practice of forcing blacks to give their seats to whites. In 1999, the 86-year-old Parks received the Congressional Gold Medal, the highest civilian honor awarded by Congress.

Dr. Martin Luther King —
© National Archives and Records Administration

*"I have a dream that one day...
the sons of former slaves and the sons of former
slaveowners will be able to sit down together
at the table of brotherhood."*

Martin Luther King, Jr., March on Washington, D.C., August 28, 1963

The Civil Rights Movement

Years after the Civil War, African Americans still suffered from racism and the heritage of slavery. The 1896 Supreme Court case *Plessy v. Ferguson* declared the common practice of segregation legal as long as blacks and whites had public facilities that were "separate but equal." In reality, the facilities and protections for black citizens were never equal to those for whites. On May 17, 1954, voting on a Kansas case *(Brown v. Board of Education)* brought by the National Association for the Advancement of Colored People (NAACP), the Supreme Court ruled unanimously that racially seg-

Civil Rights March on Washington, DC —
© National Archives and Records Administration

regated schools were "inherently unequal." This landmark case—and the Southern states' deliberate slowness in complying—is generally viewed as the beginning of the modern civil rights movement. From 1954 to 1969, thousands of activists, both black and white, held boycotts, sit-ins, street marches and rallies. The Southern Christian Leadership Conference (SCLC), organized by Dr. King, helped black churches and communities all over the South organize nonviolent protests and raise funds for a widespread fight against segregation. Public outcry led Congress to pass the Civil Rights Act of 1964, which outlawed racial discrimination in any form and the 1965 Voting Rights Act, which eliminated poll taxes and literacy tests used to prevent blacks from registering to vote.

Address: 400 Washington Avenue

Phone: 334-956-8200

www.splcenter.org

Colonial Williamsburg —
© Colonial Williamsburg Foundation, Williamsburg, VA

Williamsburg, Virginia

Colonial capital of Virginia in the 1700s, Williamsburg has been carefully re-created on the 173 acres where the town once sat. The restoration, started in the late 1920s and ongoing to this day, includes 88 original shops, his-

toric houses and buildings plus hundreds of reconstructed colonial structures on their original sites. History lives on in Colonial Williamsburg, where costumed guides and interpreters depict 18th-century characters going about their daily routines, and reenact events leading up to the Revolution.

Colonial Williamsburg —

Defining Moments: 1699

Williamsburg had its beginnings in 1699, when colonial legislators moved their capital inland from Jamestown to Middle Plantation, the location of the newly established College of William and Mary. The second-oldest institution of higher learning in the U.S. (Harvard is the oldest), the College of William and Mary was chartered by England's King William III and Queen Mary in 1693 as a theological college for gentlemen.

Also named for William III, the town centered along mile-long Duke of Gloucester Street, anchored on the east by the colonial capitol building, on the west by the College of William and Mary, and in the middle by Bruton Parish Church—a layout reflecting the governmental, educational and spiritual concerns of 18th-century Englishmen. Williamsburg grew quickly into a commercial, political and cultural center. Many prominent Virginians educated at the college (including Thomas Jefferson) took up the patriotic cause, and the town itself became a hotbed of Revolutionary zeal. George Washington, Thomas Jefferson, Patrick Henry and other leading figures of the American Revolution served in Virginia's House of Burgesses (British-elected representatives).

In 1780 the Virginia capital was moved to Richmond and Williamsburg languished. By the late 19th century, the colonial capital was virtually forgotten, its buildings neglected or Victorianized beyond recognition. Fortunately, in 1926, the rector of Bruton Parish Church, W.A.R. Goodwin, brought the town to the attention of philanthropist John D. Rockefeller, Jr. According to his hope "that the future may learn from the past," Rockefeller provided the funding for scholars and archaeologists to begin reconstructing the colonial town.

"Caesar...had his Brutus, Charles the First his Cromwell, and George III may profit by their example. If this be treason, make the most of it."

Patrick Henry, 1765

15

Window to America's Past
Colonial Williamsburg

Highlights of History

★ Capitol Building

Seat of colonial government, the Capitol was constructed in an H shape, symbolizing the bicameral system of British colonial government. The elected burgesses were housed on the sparely decorated east side of the building, and the royal governor and his counsel of 13 appointed men occupied the lavishly decorated west side. Here, in the general court, the council sat

Colonial Williamsburg - Capitol Building — © Colonial Williamsburg Foundation, Williamsburg, VA

in judgement of colonists accused of crimes. It was in the Hall of the House of Burgesses with its simple, straight-backed pews that patriotic firebrand Patrick Henry delivered his oft-quoted inflammatory speech in reaction to Britain's passage of the Stamp Act.

★ Raleigh Tavern

The capital's social life revolved around this lively tavern, where the likes of illustrious Virginians George Washington, Thomas Jefferson and Peyton Randolph feasted on wild game, played whist and quaffed ale. When, owing to their outspoken patriotism, Virginia's elected burgesses were dissolved by the royal governor, they reconvened unofficially at the Raleigh. Painted above the mantel of the tavern's Apollo Room is a Latin motto, which translates to mean "Jollity, the offspring of wisdom and good living."

"Hilaritas sapitentiae et bonae vitae proles."

Latin motto from the Raleigh Tavern

★ Governor's Palace

Seven royal governors from Britain and Virginia's first two independent governors lived in this manse, ranked as the most impressive colonial building of its era. From the fine woodwork and display of 18th-century firearms on the first floor to the hand-tooled Moroccan leather wall covering in the second-floor governor's office, the palace befits the status that vice royalty enjoyed in the capital of England's largest American colony. The palace ballroom hosted the city's most fashionable citizens and its most elegant social functions. During the siege of Yorktown, the structure served as a hospital for wounded Continental soldiers. Surrounding the palace are 10 acres of formal gardens, including a boxwood maze that was a favorite of colonial children.

Governor's Palace Gardens — © Colonial Williamsburg Foundation/ Virginia Tourism Corporation

Address: Major sights are located along Duke of Gloucester Street in Williamsburg

Phone: 757-229-1000

www.colonialwilliamsburg.org

Epic in Granite
Crazy Horse Memorial

Crazy Horse, South Dakota

This 563-foot mountain sculpture of Sioux chief Crazy Horse is the largest sculpture project in the world. The chief's 87-foot head (about 9 stories tall) is higher than Egypt's ancient Sphinx. His sculpted

Crazy Horse Memorial — © John Gottberg/MICHELIN

arm stretches the length of a football field. Still being worked on, the huge carving-in-progress began in 1948 after Sioux leaders asked sculptor Korczak Ziolkowski to create a memorial in the Black Hills of South Dakota that would complement Mount Rushmore, located 17 miles northeast. When completed, the sculpture will show the chief mounted on his horse.

Defining Moments: 1948

Korczak Ziolkowski (1908–1982) detonated the first blast on the 600-foot mountain in June 1948. He had to climb 741 steps to the area where he carved, sometimes going up and down several times a day to service an old compressor. By 1965 work had progressed on the sculpture's head, arm and the horse's mane. In 1998, the chief's head was finally finished. Ziolkowski's widow and children are carrying on the work today.

"My lands are where my dead lie buried."

Crazy Horse, 1877

Crazy Horse was born near Rapid City, South Dakota around 1842. He became one of the fiercest warriors in defending his Sioux people and their territory. When gold

was discovered in the Black Hills in 1874, the large Indian reservation there was overwhelmed with prospectors who disregarded Sioux treaty rights. With the Cheyenne, Crazy Horse and his men attacked General George Crook's army, forcing Crook to end his pursuit of the chief. Then he joined Chief Sitting Bull's Sioux encampment farther north and, in 1876, helped annihilate Lieutenant Colonel George Custer's battalion of U.S. soldiers along the Little Bighorn River. Crazy Horse died in 1877 at Fort Robinson in Nebraska, reportedly killed in a scuffle involving a knife.

© John Gottberg/MICHELIN

These words are being carved on the mountain in letters three feet tall:

WHEN THE COURSE OF HISTORY HAS BEEN TO LET THESE TRUTHS HERE CARVED BE KNOWN: CONSCIENCE DICTATES CIVILIZATIONS LIVE AND DUTY OURS TO PLACE BEFORE THE WORLD, A CHRONICLE WHICH WILL LONG ENDURE. FOR LIKE ALL THINGS UNDER US AND BEYOND INEVITABLY WE MUST PASS INTO OBLIVION. THIS LAND OF REFUGE TO THE STRANGER WAS OURS FOR COUNTLESS EONS BEFORE: CIVILIZATIONS MAJESTIC AND MIGHTY. OUR GIFTS WERE MANY WHICH WE SHARED AND GRATITUDE FOR THEM WAS KNOWN. BUT LATER, GIVEN MY OPPRESSED ONES WERE MURDER, RAPE AND SANGUINE WAR. LOOKING EAST FROM WHENCE INVADERS CAME, GREEDY USURPERS OF OUR HERITAGE. FOR US THE PAST IS IN OUR HEARTS, THE FUTURE NEVER TO BE FULFILLED. TO YOU I GIVE THIS GRANITE EPIC FOR YOUR DESCENDANTS TO ALWAYS KNOW—'MY LANDS ARE WHERE MY DEAD LIE BURIED.'

Korczak Ziolkowski, Sculptor, Crazy Horse Memorial, Black Hills, S.D.

Address: U.S. Highway 16/385, 4 miles north of Custer

Phone: 605-673-4681

www.crazyhorse.org

Icon of American Enterprise
Empire State Building

New York, New York

Rising to a height of 1,454 feet with a grace and strength that have made it one of the finest and most breathtaking skyscrapers ever built, the Empire State Building has remained, since its completion in 1931, the most distinctive feature of the Manhattan skyline. At night, the top 30 stories are illuminated, often in colors that celebrate a national holiday, like red, white and blue for July 4th.

Empire State Building and Chrysler Building
© Jon Ortner / NYC & Company, Inc.

Defining Moments: 1931

Financed by a corporation headed by former New York governor Alfred E. Smith, the skyscraper was completed in May 1931, less than two years after excavations began in 1929. Work progressed at an incredible pace; at times, the building rose more than a floor each day. Since there are only two stories of foundations, 60,000 tons of steel beams—enough to lay a double-track railroad from New York to Baltimore—were added to support the tower. On clear days, views extend 80 miles from the 86th- and 102nd-floor observatories.

Empire State Building
© Joseph Pobereskin / NYC & Company, Inc.

Address: 350 Fifth Avenue, corner of Fifth Avenue and West 34th Street

Phone: 212-736-3100

www.esbnyc.org

First U.S. Capitol
Federal Hall

★★★★★★★★

Federal Hall © National Park Service

New York, New York

Located in lower Manhattan in the Financial District, Federal Hall National Memorial commemorates the place where George Washington took the oath of office as the first U.S. president and where the amendments known as the Bill of Rights were first proposed. New York's City Hall was remodeled in 1789 to serve as Federal Hall, the nation's first capitol building, until the federal government moved to Philadelphia.

Defining Moments: 1789

George Washington took the oath on the balcony of Federal Hall on April 30, 1789. In June 1789, Virginian James Madison proposed several amendments to the Constitution while serving in the House of Representatives, which convened in Federal Hall. Ten of his amendments were approved by 1791 and have since become known as the Bill of Rights, guarantees of important liberties such as freedom of speech and freedom of the press. Federal Hall was eventually torn down, but the site and its present building were designated a national memorial in 1955. A bronze statue of George Washington stands at the top of the wide steps leading to the entrance.

Address: 26 Wall Street

Phone: 212-825-6888

www.nps.gov/feha

★★★★★★★★

Fort Stanwix — © National Park Service

Rome, New York

During the War of Independence, this palisaded stronghold near the Mohawk River came under siege for 21 days in August 1777, when the British attempted a three-legged strategy to cut New England off from the southern colonies. The fort's American forces stood their ground until rumors of approaching Continental reinforcements, among other factors, caused the British to retreat. The siege was a failure, as was the entire British campaign in the region: the Mohawk Valley remained unconquered. Today a national monument, Fort Stanwix has been reconstructed to appear as it did in 1777.

Defining Moments: 1777

The original wood and sod fort was built by the British in 1758 during the French and Indian War (1756–1763). By war's end, the British had all but abandoned the outpost. The Americans, having rebuilt and renamed the dilapidated fort, successfully defended it against the British during the Revolution. The fort saw little military action after that, and in 1781 the barracks burned down. The National Park Service maintains the reconstructed fort, which bears its original name.

Address: Intersection of Routes 365, 49, 46 and 69

Phone: 315-336-2090

www.nps.gov

Prelude to Larger Victory
Fort Ticonderoga

★★★★★★★★★

Ticonderoga, New York

Strategically located above 125-mile-long Lake Champlain, "Fort Ti" is famous for the surprise pre-dawn attack launched here against the British in May 1775 by Revolutionaries Ethan Allen and his Green Mountain Boys of Vermont, and Benedict Arnold and his men. The supplies captured from the fort, including 59 cannons, were used the following spring by George Washington and his men to drive the British out of Boston.

Fort Ticonderoga overlooking Lake Champlain and Mount Defiance

Defining Moments: 1775

Built by the French to defend the southeast border of their fur-trade empire, the star-shaped, stone-and-log fort was captured by the British in 1759, the French deliberately blowing it up as they withdrew. Having rebuilt and renamed the fort Ticonderoga (a Mohawk word for "place between the waters"), the Redcoats held it until May 10, 1775 when "colonial rabble" heroically raided the fortress. Reconstruction began in 1908, incorporating the old fort's ruins.

Fort Ticonderoga's Fife & Drum Corps
©Fort Ticonderoga Museum

Address: Route 74, one mile east of the village of Ticonderoga

Phone: 518-585-2821

www.fort-ticonderoga.org

Waymarks of Independence
Freedom Trail

Paul Revere Statue © photodisc

Boston, Massachusetts

The Freedom Trail is a three-mile walking tour linking 16 major colonial and Revolutionary sites in the Boston area. Indicated on the pavement by a red brick line, or painted red stripe, the trail begins at Boston Common and leads through downtown, the North End, and finally to Charlestown. The Old State House, Paul Revere House, the Old North Church and Bunker Hill Monument are especially significant among the trail's historic sites.

Listen, my children, and you shall hear
Of the midnight ride of Paul Revere,
On the eighteenth of April, in Seventy-five;
Hardly a man is now alive
Who remembers that famous day and year.
He said to his friend, 'If the British march
By land or sea from the town to-night,
Hang a lantern aloft in the belfry arch
Of the North Church tower as a signal light,
One, if by land, and two, if by sea;
And I on the opposite shore will be,
Ready to ride and spread the alarm....'

Paul Revere's Ride,
Henry Wadsworth Longfellow, 1861

Waymarks of Independence
Freedom Trail

★ The Old State House

Boston's oldest public building (1713), the State House originally served as headquarters of the British government. On March 5, 1770, a group of Bostonians gathered near the State House to protest British policy. When a British officer answered the insults of a protester with the butt of his musket, the crowd became abusive and the guard was called out. Provoked by the civilians, several Redcoats fired their weapons, killing five men. This tragic event, known thereafter as the Boston Massacre, helped rally the colonists against the British. Two weeks after the Declaration of Independence was adopted in Philadelphia on July 4, 1776, the document was read from the balcony of the State House.

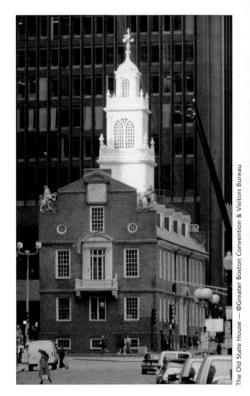

The Old State House — ©Greater Boston Convention & Visitors Bureau

★ Paul Revere House

In the North End of the city sits a two-and-a-half-story wooden house, the only structure in downtown Boston that remains from the 17th century. Already 90 years old when silversmith Paul Revere bought it in 1770, the small residence was the starting point of Revere's historic ride to Lexington on April 18, 1775, to forewarn the colonists of the approach of 800 British soldiers. The British had been dispatched to seize the colonists' stash of arms in the outlying towns of Lexington and Concord and to arrest

Paul Revere House ©The Freedom Trail

Patriot leaders John Hancock and Samuel Adams, who were hiding there. According to a prearranged plan, on the night the British left, the caretaker of Old North Church displayed two lanterns in the steeple to signal their departure from Boston by boat (one lantern would have signaled that the British were approaching by land).

★ Old North Church

It was in this Boston church in the North End on the evening of April 18, 1775, that the caretaker displayed two lanterns in the steeple to warn of the departure of the British from Boston by boat across the Charles River to Cambridge, en route to Lexington. Less than a century later, the church was immortalized by Henry Wadsworth Longfellow in his poem, Paul Revere's Ride. Old North, now Christ Church, was built in 1723.

★ Bunker Hill Monument

Across Boston Harbor in Charlestown rises the Bunker Hill Monument, a 221-foot granite obelisk that marks the site of the Battle of Bunker Hill in 1775. Here 1,500 militiamen valiantly confronted 5,000 British troops in an effort to save the city.

The Siege of Boston and the Battle of Bunker Hill

After the events at Lexington and Concord, the British retreated to Boston, where they were surrounded by rebel forces. While the British eyed the strategic heights around Boston, colonial leaders, informed of the British plan to fortify Bunker Hill in Charlestown, hastened to occupy nearby Breed's Hill before the arrival of the British. On June 17, 1775, when the British awoke and discovered an American stronghold had been built on Breed's Hill during the night, 5,000 soldiers were sent out to capture the site. Although the colonists' position was defended by only 1,500 militiamen, the British failed in their first two attempts to secure the fort. They then set fire to Charlestown and launched a third attack against the rebels. Colonial leader William Prescott, aware that his men were low on ammunition, gave his famous order: "Don't fire until you see the whites of their eyes!" The British finally captured the fort, but in doing so, they lost over 10 percent of all the British officers killed during the Revolution. This struggle is mistakenly known as the Battle of Bunker Hill, since it actually took place on Breed's Hill.

Bunker Hill Monument — ©FayFoto/Greater Boston Convention & Visitors Bureau/ BostonUSA.com

Address: Downtown Boston, the North End and Charlestown

Phone: 617-242-5642

www.thefreedomtrail.org

12
Symbol of Westward Expansion
Gateway Arch

★★★★★★★★

St. Louis, Missouri

This 630-foot bend of steel is the tallest man-made monument in the United States. Located in downtown St. Louis, the arch stands at the edge of the Mississippi River, the great waterway that transported pioneers heading for the vast Louisiana Purchase, which the U.S., under President Thomas Jefferson, bought from France in 1803. The arch symbolizes the opening of the American West and the young

Gateway Arch — © Missouri Division of Tourism

nation's expansion toward the Pacific Ocean. A tribute as well to human ingenuity and engineering, the arch is synonymous with the city of St. Louis.

Defining Moments: 1965

The arch is officially part of the Jefferson National Expansion Memorial in honor of President Jefferson and his vision of a continental United States. Designed by architect Eero Saarinen, the structure was completed in 1965 for under $15 million. Its precarious construction, size and shimmering stainless-steel exterior leave spectators awestruck. Inside, tram cars ascend the curve of each leg to the apex, where small portholes provide the best views of the city. By law, no building in St. Louis may exceed the monument's height.

Address: Riverfront between Poplar and Washington Avenues

Phone: 877-982-1410

www.stlouisarch.com

Gettysburg — © National Park Service

Gettysburg, Pennsylvania

In July 1863 this crossroads town witnessed the worst carnage of the Civil War: 28,000 Confederate and 23,000 Union casualties in three days. Five months later, the town was the backdrop for one of the most revered speeches in U.S. history—Abraham Lincoln's Gettysburg Address. Today the battlefield has been preserved in 5,900-acre Gettysburg National Military Park, where more than 1,300 monuments honor the brave men from both North and South who fought here.

Defining Moments: 1863

In spring 1863, General Robert E. Lee, commander of the Army of Northern Virginia, decided to invade the North, hoping to capture Pennsylvania's state capital of Harrisburg. Recent losses at Chancellorsville and Fredericksburg, Virginia, had demoralized the Union army. To counter Lee, Union commander Major General Joe Hooker slowly moved

Tragedy and Turning Point
Gettysburg

© National Park Service

his Army of the Potomac north. Neither general expected the collision that began on July 1, when two Confederate divisions entered Gettysburg. After a Union sentinel spotted them, a skirmish broke out. As the fighting intensified, Hooker was replaced by Major General George Meade, who would command 93,000 Union troops against 75,000 Confederates during the three-day battle.

© National Park Service

At the end of the first day, the Confederates had the upper hand. But on July 2 the battle turned. By July 3 Lee realized that desperate measures were necessary. That afternoon, 12,000 Confederates under General George Pickett attacked the Union position on Cemetery Ridge. As the Rebels surged across open fields, they were mowed down by Union fire. Pickett's Charge cost the Confederacy 6,000 men. The following day, Lee ordered a retreat. Never again would his army launch an offensive on northern soil; it was the beginning of the end of the Southern cause.

The Gettysburg Address

Four score and seven years ago our fathers brought forth on this continent a new nation conceived in Liberty, and dedicated to the proposition that all men are created equal. Now we are engaged in a great civil war, testing whether that nation or any nation so conceived and so dedicated, can long endure. We are met on a great battle-field of that war. We have come to dedicate a portion of that field, as a final resting place for those who here gave their lives that that nation might live. It is altogether fitting and proper that we should do this. But, in a larger sense, we can not dedicate—we can not consecrate—we can not hallow—this ground. The brave men, living and dead, who struggled here, have consecrated it, far above our poor power to add or detract. The world will little note, nor long remember what we say here, but it can never forget what they did here. It is for us the living, rather, to be dedicated here to the unfinished work which they who fought here have thus far so nobly advanced. It is rather for us to be here dedicated to the great task remaining before us—that from these honored dead we take increased devotion to that cause for which they gave the last full measure of devotion—that we here highly resolve that these dead shall not have died in vain—that this nation, under God, shall have a new birth of freedom—and that government of the people, by the people, for the people, shall not perish from the earth.

Abraham Lincoln, November 19, 1863

Funds were solicited to create a national cemetery on the site. At its dedication on November 19, 1863, popular orator Edward Everett spoke for two hours. Then President Lincoln, who had been asked to add a "few appropriate remarks," rose and began his brief, stirring words, now so familiar to Americans.

© National Park Service

Address: 97 Taneytown Road

Phone: 717-334-1124

www.nps.gov/gett

Gateway to Opportunity
Golden Gate Bridge

★★★★★★★★

Golden Gate Bridge ©PhotoDisc

San Francisco, California

Spanning the merging waters of San Francisco Bay and the Pacific Ocean some 220 feet above the highest tide, this bright orange suspension bridge is a beloved San Francisco symbol. It stands as a powerful metaphor for golden opportunity to the thousands who enter the United States from the western shore.

Defining Moments: 1937

After years of wrangling over the proposed bridge, groundbreaking took place in January 1933. During construction, chief engineer Joseph Strauss, who had built 400 bridges, enforced unprecedented safety measures that have since become standard. Loss of life, though tragic, was limited to 11 workers; the bridge, built at a cost of $35 million, was hailed as a model of safety and economy. On inauguration day, May 27, 1937, more than 200,000 people walked across the 1.22-mile span. It remained the world's longest suspension bridge until 1964.

Address: Access from US-101 or from Lincoln Boulevard

Phone: 415-921-5858

www.goldengatebridge.org

Hoover Dam ©PhotoDisc

Boulder City, Nevada

At 726 feet Hoover Dam, located about 30 miles southeast of Las Vegas, is the highest dam in the Western Hemisphere. Stretching across the Black Canyon of the Colorado River, it was constructed in 1936 when Lake Mead—North America's largest, deepest reservoir—was created, adding 700 miles of shoreline to the Nevada-Arizona border. Named for U.S. president Herbert Hoover, the dam was built for flood control, electricity, recreation and irrigation.

Defining Moments: 1936

In 1932 four tunnels were bored through canyon walls to divert the river. Two cofferdams were built; the construction area was pumped dry and excavated to bedrock. In 1935, two years ahead of schedule, the last concrete was poured and in 1936, the dam began operations. The project came in under budget, but 96 construction workers died. Until 1949, it was the world's largest hydroelectric dam.

Address: From Boulder City, follow Buchanan Street for 11 miles

Phone: 702-294-3517

www.usbr.gov/lc/hooverdam

Icon of Self-Government
Independence Hall

Philadelphia, Pennsylvania

Some of the most important moments in the nation's history occurred in this 107-foot-long, steepled brick building, from whose belfry the Liberty Bell sounded the call of freedom for nearly 100 years. It was here, on July 4, 1776, that the Declaration of Independence was officially adopted, setting the colonies upon a new course toward self-government. In 1787 the U.S. Constitution—the laws of the federal government and the rights of the nation's citizens—was also adopted here. Today Independence Hall is preserved as a monument to the hard-won liberties that Americans hold so dear.

Independence Hall with group
©Philadelphia Convention & Visitors Bureau/ photographer: Jim McWilliams

Defining Moments: 1756

The building was completed in 1756 as the Pennsylvania State House. Following the battles at Lexington and Concord in April 1775, delegates of the Second Continental Congress convened in the State House on May 10 of that year to determine how the colonies should respond to increasing hostilities with Britain. As reports of warfare spread, members of Congress adopted an aggressive stance toward the Crown. In June they appointed Virginia delegate George Washington as commander in chief of the Continental army—a job which he accepted without pay. Back in Britain, King George III proclaimed the colonists to be in "open and avowed rebellion." The Revolutionary War had begun.

In June 1776, the Continental

Congress met again in the State House, where Virginia delegate Richard Henry Lee presented a resolution for independence from Britain. After two days of debate, the resolution was tabled for several weeks while a committee, headed by Thomas Jefferson, worked to draft a declaration explaining why such a resolution was necessary. The resulting Declaration of Independence was adopted on July 4 and read aloud outside the hall in Independence Square on July 8.

Independence Hall Interior
©Nick Kelsh/ Philadelphia Convention & Visitors Bureau

"We hold these truths to be self-evident, that all men are created equal, that they are endowed by their Creator with certain unalienable Rights, that among these are Life, Liberty and the pursuit of Happiness."

From the Declaration of Independence, 1776

Throughout the Revolutionary War, the Second Continental Congress continued to convene here, and in 1781, when independence at last seemed imminent, Congress approved the Articles of Confederation as a governing document for the newly created United States. On September 17, 1787, the delegates of the Constitutional Convention met in the State House chambers to adopt the U.S. Constitution for their young nation.

The building owes its current name to Revolutionary War hero the Marquis de Lafayette, who in 1824 focused attention on the historic significance of what he called the "Hall of Independence."

Key Figures
★★★★★★★
Thomas Jefferson (1743–1826)
George Washington (1732–1799)
Richard Henry Lee (1732–1794)

Address: Chestnut Street between 5th and 6th Streets

Phone: 215-965-2305

www.nps.gov/inde

Seed of a New Nation
Jamestown

Jamestown Settlement ©PhotoDisc

Jamestown, Virginia

The 1,500-acre island in the James River, about six miles south of Williamsburg, became the site of the first permanent English-speaking colony in America in 1607, 13 years before the Mayflower landed at Plymouth. In 1619 Jamestown was the setting for the beginnings of representative government in North America. The foundations that took root here helped mold the nation that would become the United States of America.

"A verie fit place for the erecting of a great cittie...."

John Smith, 1608

Defining Moments: 1607

On May 13, 1607, three English vessels with 104 colonists on board anchored in the James River. The colonists began building a wooden fort for defense and named the capital of their colony after King James I, who had granted their charter. By summer they were starving, but under the leadership of Captain John Smith and with help from the local Powhatan Indians, who taught the colonists how to grow corn, the plucky colony survived. In 1609 some 400 additional settlers arrived. By the following year, hunger, disease, and a harsh winter had reduced the population of the settlement by two thirds.

Eventually, the cultivation of tobacco ensured the colony's success. In 1619 elected burgesses met in the church at Jamestown, the first representative English government in the continent. Despite many setbacks, the settlement grew to become the capital of the royal colony of Virginia, a distinction it held until 1698, when the colonial government relocated to Williamsburg. Now part of Colonial National Historical Park, Jamestown National Historic Site preserves the tidewater land where the capital once flourished. Nearby, Jamestown Settlement re-creates the settlers' early fort, the three ships that carried the colonists to the New World, and a Powhatan Indian village.

Pocahontas

Pocahontas ("the playful one"), one of the most well-known Native American women, was actually Matoaka, the daughter of a powerful Powhatan chief. She was reputedly intrigued by the English colonists and rescued their leader, John Smith, when her father threatened to kill him. In 1614 Pocahontas married John Rolfe, the colonist responsible for hybridizing a smokable form of tobacco. Their marriage led to four years of harmony between the native Powhatans and the colonists—a period called the Pocahontas Peace. In 1616 the couple sailed with their infant son to England, where Pocahontas became the toast of the English court. Sadly, on their return to America, the 29-year-old Indian woman died. She was buried on English soil.

Address: West end of the Colonial Parkway

Phone: 757-229-1733

www.nps.gov/jame

Monument to Genius
Jefferson Memorial

Washington, D.C.

Occupying a peaceful spot on the south shore of the Tidal Basin, rimmed with its famous cherry trees, the Jefferson Memorial commemorates the nation's third president. Rudulph Evans' 19-foot bronze statue of Jefferson, holding a rolled parchment on which the Declaration of Independence is written, dominates the open-air interior. Inscribed on four wall panels, Jefferson's

Jefferson Memorial

writings—including portions of the Declaration, his admonitions against slavery, and his convictions regarding religious freedom and flexibility in government—capture the visionary greatness and powerful eloquence of this Renaissance man.

Defining Moments: 1934

In 1934 Congress authorized the building of the Jefferson Memorial to join the city's

Jefferson Memorial ©PhotoDisc

existing monuments honoring U.S. presidents Washington (1888) and Lincoln (1922). Acknowledging Jefferson's love of classical architecture, John Russell Pope, architect of several buildings in the capital city, designed a 20th-century interpretation of Rome's ancient Pantheon. His memorial to Jefferson is aligned on an axis with the White House at the west end of Washington's grassy, museum-lined Mall, where the memorial commands a striking view that enhances its emotional impact.

*"No man shall be compelled to frequent
or support any religious worship
or ministry or shall otherwise suffer on account of his religious
opinions or belief."*

Thomas Jefferson

Serving the New Nation

Statesman, architect, musician, inventor, horticulturalist, philosopher and president, Thomas Jefferson (1743–1826) was one of the country's great geniuses. He helped to formulate the young nation's system of government, plan its capital city and develop such fundamental principles as public education and religious freedom. His historic conflict with secretary of the Treasury Alexander Hamilton on the power of state versus federal government under the Constitution led to the formation of a two-party political system.

After studying law for five years, Jefferson practiced on his own for seven. In 1769 he was elected to the House of Burgesses and participated in the colonists' protests against British taxation without representation. In 1774 he was elected to the First Continental Congress in Philadelphia. At the Second Continental Congress a year later, he was appointed to a committee to draft a statement to the British Crown that justified the colonists' stand on independence. Fellow committee members encouraged Jefferson to draft the document himself, known as he was for eloquent writing. On July 4, 1776, his Declaration of Independence was signed by the Continental Congress. Jefferson served as vice president under John Adams from 1797 to 1801 before becoming the country's third president (1801–1809).

Address: South bank of the Tidal Basin

Phone: 202-426-6841

www.nps.gov/nacc

Testament to Technology
Kennedy Space Center

Rocket Garden
©Kennedy Space Center Visitor Complex

Merritt Island, Florida

Home to the nation's space program, Florida's East Coast near Titusville has witnessed the emergence of the world's most sophisticated technology. Every U.S. rocket—from the one that carried the Explorer I satellite in 1958 to today's space shuttles—has blasted off from Merritt Island or adjoining Cape Canaveral, 50 miles east of Orlando. Covering 84,000 acres, Kennedy Space Center encompasses two launch pads, one of the world's longest runways, and the Vehicle Assembly Building—large enough to hold nearly four Empire State Buildings laid end-to-end. At the Visitor Complex, bus tours enable the public to access otherwise restricted areas of the facility and take a scenic drive out to Cape Canaveral to see facilities where the first manned space flights, and more recent probes, were launched.

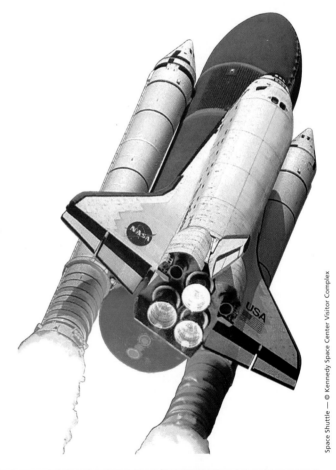

Defining Moments: 1962

Rocket launches from the beginning of the American space program up to 1964 took place only at Cape Canaveral Air Force Station (called Cape Kennedy from 1963–1973), which had been used by the U.S. Air Force since 1950 as the test site for long-range guided missiles. Both the Soviet Union and the U.S. announced their intentions in 1955 of launching artificial satellites; the Soviets took the first step, deploying two Sputnik satellites in late 1957. The following year, on January 31, 1958, the U.S. launched its first satellite. In October of that year, NASA was created. After President Kennedy challenged the nation in May 1961 "to achieve the goal, before the decade is out, of landing a man on the moon and returning him safely to Earth," NASA began buying up land on Merritt Island for its main launch facility. Opened in 1962 as the National Aeronautics and Space Administration (NASA) Launch Operations Center, the complex was renamed in President John F. Kennedy's honor after his assassination in 1963.

"That's one small step for man, one giant leap for mankind."

Astronaut Neil Armstrong walking on the moon, July 1969

Space Shuttle — © Kennedy Space Center Visitor Complex

Address: Route 405 (NASA Parkway), off US-1

Phone: 321-449-4444

www.kennedyspacecenter.com

Heroic Journey of Discovery
Lewis and Clark Trail

Kaw Point near Kansas City
© Teresa Garrison/ Kansas Lewis and Clark Bicentennial Commission

St. Louis, Missouri to the Pacific Ocean

President Thomas Jefferson commissioned a geographic and scientific expedition to explore the Louisiana Purchase, the vast lands newly purchased by the U.S. from France in 1803. The leaders of the expedition—Meriwether Lewis and William Clark—have forever since been linked in American minds. Their Corps of Discovery set off from St. Louis on May 14, 1804. It returned 28 months later, on September 23, 1806, after traveling more than 8,000 miles up the Missouri River, across the Rocky Mountains, down the Snake and Columbia Rivers to the Pacific Ocean, and back again. Though not the first to reach the Pacific overland from the east, they succeeded in making the unknown known to a growing nation and opening the gates to further exploration and settlement. Today, the Lewis and Clark National Historic Trail, traversing 11 states, commemorates their epic journey from Illinois and Missouri through Kansas, Iowa, Nebraska, the Dakotas, Montana, Idaho, Oregon and Washington.

Defining Moments: 1804

Jefferson gained congressional approval for a military expedition to explore the Louisiana territory and find a route to the Pacific Ocean. He selected his personal secretary, Meriwether Lewis (1774–1809), to head the expedition. Lewis asked his boyhood friend, career soldier William Clark (1770–1838) to serve as co-leader. With orders to promote trade with the Indians, observe flora and fauna, map major rivers and record soils and climate, the 33 trained frontiersmen and their leaders set course up the Missouri River in 1804.

Sacagawea (c.1786–1812), a Shoshone woman, was instrumental in obtaining horses for the explorers when

Lewis and Clark Statue
© Missouri Division of Tourism

the expedition encountered a Shoshone tribe, led by her own brother. After an arduous journey that included a trek over the Rockies, Lewis and Clark arrived at the Pacific Ocean on November 7, 1805. Their mission accomplished, they returned with their men to St. Louis in September 1806, having lost only one man, to illness.

Today the famous trail is geographically and historically spectacular in many places.

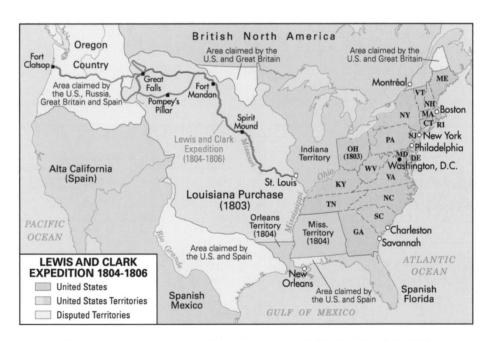

LEWIS AND CLARK
EXPEDITION 1804-1806
- United States
- United States Territories
- Disputed Territories

Address: L & C National Historic Trail Office, Omaha, Nebraska

Phone: 402-661-1804

www.nps.gov/lecl

Confrontations of Consequence
Lexington and Concord

Old North Bridge, Concord — © National Park Service

Lexington and Concord, Massachusetts

In the minds of many Americans, Lexington has been historically linked with Concord since April 19, 1775. On that date, British and colonial troops clashed in these towns, triggering the events that exploded into the American Revolution and changed forever the course of U.S. history. Minute Man National Historical Park commemorates those historic events and the men who lost their lives here.

Defining Moments: 1775

Tensions between the colonists and the British increased steadily following the passage in 1765 of the Stamp Act, a direct tax levied by the British on the American colonies without their consent. In 1774 the colonists established their own legislative body, the Provincial Congress, with John Hancock as its president. Within a year the Congress had created a militia and stockpiled arms in Concord for the colonial troops. England reacted swiftly by dispatching soldiers to Boston and closing the city's port. In an attempt to end rebel activity, General Thomas Gage, leader of the British forces in Boston, decided to march on Concord and seize the weapons hidden there.

"By the rude bridge that arched the flood,
Their flag to April's breeze unfurled,
Here once the embattled farmers stood,
And fired the shot heard round the world."

Ralph Waldo Emerson, Concord Hymn, 1836

Forewarned by Paul Revere of the approach of the British, 77 patriots had spent the night of April 18, 1775, in Lexington, waiting for the enemy. As they assembled before dawn, their leader, Captain John Parker, advised them: "Stand your ground and don't fire unless fired upon, but if they mean to have a war, let it begin here!" At about five o'clock in the morning, 700 British soldiers began to arrive, and Parker, realizing that his men were greatly outnumbered, gave the order to disperse. He was too late: a shot rang out, and during the skirmish that followed, 8 patriots were killed and 10 wounded. The British commander ordered his men to regroup and march on to Concord.

In Concord, patriots observed the approaching British soldiers from a hilltop. They also saw smoke from the enemy's torching of militia supplies. Fearful that the British would burn Concord, the colonists advanced to the Old North Bridge. There, the untrained, poorly equipped farmers—called "minutemen" because of their readiness to take up arms at a

Minute Man National Park — © National Park Service

minute's notice—stood their ground against the Redcoats and returned the enemy's volley. Outnumbered, the British, weary and reduced in numbers, retreated to Boston along Battle Road, exposed to the sniper fire of minutemen hiding behind walls and trees. At Lexington, the British rested and received reinforcements. Near what is now Arlington, intense fighting involving some 5,000 men broke out. In all, the confrontations cost the British 73 lives and 174 wounded, while the Americans counted 49 dead and 40 wounded. Today a replica of the historic bridge arches the Concord River.

Address: Minute Man National Historical Park. 174 Liberty Street, Concord

Phone: 978-369-6993

www.nps.gov/mima

America's Herald of Freedom
Liberty Bell

Philadelphia, Pennsylvania

Recognized as the national symbol of freedom, America's revered Liberty Bell is permanently on display in Philadelphia's Independence National Historical Park. The 2,000-pound copper bell's finest moment occurred on July 8, 1776, when it was rung to announce the first public reading of the Declaration of Independence from the Yard of the State House (now Independence Hall). From 1753 to 1846, the famed bell summoned people to assemble or tolled in recognition of historic events, such as the convening of the First Continental Congress in 1774.

Liberty Bell, Independence NHP — ©Philadelphia Convention & Visitors Bureau/ photographer: Anthony Sinagoga

Defining Moments: 1751

In 1751 the speaker of the Pennsylvania Assembly ordered a bell to be cast by a London foundry, possibly to commemorate the 50th anniversary of William Penn's Charter of Privileges granted to citizens of his colony. Soon after its arrival in Philadelphia, the bell developed a crack, and local metalsmiths John Pass and John Stow recast it using metal from the original bell as well as copper (to make it less brittle and less prone to cracking). Their names now appear prominently on its face.

The massive bell was installed in the belfry of the State House in 1753 and was rung for official occasions for almost 100 years, until another crack again threatened its further use. Just before the British occupied Philadelphia in 1777, the bell was removed and hidden in a church in another town, so it would not be melted down to make cannons. In 1846, in commemoration of George Washington's birthday, the repaired bell sounded its last public notes, having developed another crack. The bell gained its modern name in the mid-19th century, when American abolitionists proclaimed it the "Liberty Bell" and adopted it as the symbol for their campaign to abolish slavery.

"Proclaim Liberty throughout all the Land unto all the inhabitants thereof." (Leviticus 25:10)

Biblical inscription on the Liberty Bell

In the late 1800s, in an effort to unify the country after the Civil War, the bell was toured around the country as an icon of the nation. The Liberty Bell made a final trip in 1915, returning home to Philadelphia, where it remains a silent herald of freedom.

Liberty Bell Facts

★ Weight of bell: 2,000 pounds

★ Composition: 70% copper, 25% tin, with small amounts of lead, zinc, arsenic, gold and silver

★ Circumference around the lip: 12 feet

★ Weight of clapper: 44.5 pounds

★ Length of visible fracture: 2 feet, 4 inches

★ Weight of the elm yolk: 200 pounds

Address: Market Street between 5th and 6th Streets

Phone: 215-965-2305

www.nps.gov/inde

Lincoln Memorial ©PhotoDisc

Washington, D.C.

From this stately memorial, the famous marble likeness of a seated, brooding Abraham Lincoln stares across the Reflecting Pool to the Washington Monument and the Capitol beyond. The country's 16th president—the self-educated son of a poor Kentucky farmer—is remembered as "Honest Abe," as the Great Emancipator who ultimately freed the country of slavery, and as the president who fought a civil war to keep the nation intact.

Defining Moments: 1922

Two years after Lincoln's death in 1865, a congressional commission was established to plan a monument in his memory. After decades of proposals, work finally began on the site in 1914. It was dedicated in 1922 in a ceremony attended by Robert Todd Lincoln, the president's only surviving son.

The monument's designer, Henry Bacon, produced his version of a classic temple that recalls the Parthenon in Athens, Greece. Thirty-six Doric columns form a colonnade around the structure, symbolizing the states in the Union at the time of Lincoln's death in 1865. On the southwest side, Arlington Memorial Bridge serves as a sym-

---

Lincoln Memorial ©PhotoDisc

...bolic link between Lincoln and the South's great hero, Robert E. Lee, whose home, Arlington House, overlooks the monument from the Virginia bluffs. American sculptor Daniel Chester French's massive marble statue of Lincoln, 19 feet high, captures the force of the man himself. The right wall is inscribed with Lincoln's second inaugural address. The Gettysburg Address (1863), the celebrated oratory that begins with the oft-quoted words "Four score and seven years ago," is chiseled into the left wall.

Preserver of the Union

Abraham Lincoln was faced with a nation in turmoil even before he took office in 1861. South Carolina seceded from the Union shortly after he was elected. Other southern states quickly followed suit. The month after Lincoln's inauguration, Confederate and Union troops exchanged fire at Fort Sumter, South Carolina. For the next four years, Lincoln waged a war to bring the Southern states back into the Union. In 1863 he issued his Emancipation Proclamation decreeing that slaves in the Confederate states would thereafter be free. Though this was more a symbolic gesture than a real reversal of slavery nationwide, it helped set the stage for the eventual passage in 1865 of the 13th Amendment to the Constitution, which abolished slavery. At the start of Lincoln's second term, Robert E. Lee surrendered to Ulysses S. Grant at Appomattox Court House, Virginia. With the long war over, the president turned his thoughts to reconstruction of the South, but on April 14, 1865—five days after Lee's surrender—Lincoln was shot at Ford's Theatre by the actor John Wilkes Booth. The following day, at age 56, President Abraham Lincoln died of his wounds.

Address: The Mall at 23rd Street N.W.

Phone: 202-426-6841

www.nps.gov/nacc

Ancient National Treasure
Mesa Verde

Mesa Verde National Park — © National Park Service

Mancos, Colorado

Tucked within the sheltered alcoves of the buff-colored canyon walls in the San Juan Mountains, elaborate stone villages survive to tell the story of their ancient inhabitants. Raised on canyon shelves for protection from marauders, these communities were abandoned more than seven centuries ago. Among the best-preserved archaeological sites in the Southwest, the foremost cliff dwellings in the world are contained within Mesa Verde National Park, which has been designated a UNESCO World Heritage Site for its outstanding cultural significance. It was the first U.S. national park to preserve the works of mankind (as opposed to nature).

Defining Moments: 1906

This high mountain region in Colorado's southwestern corner was once the dwelling place of Native Americans known as the Anasazi (Navajo for "ancient ones"). Thought

© National Park Service

to be descendants of the Pueblo, these early people excelled at basketry, pottery-making and stone masonry. Between AD 600 and 1300, they built cities on the mesas—natural flat-topped elevations—and within canyon alcoves. A 26-year drought and invading Navajo and Apache tribes are believed to be responsible for the departure of the Anasazi by 1300. Much later, pioneers seeking gold came to the San Juans, and mining towns sprang up in the 19th century. In the mid-1870s, government survey team members saw the dwellings, but ranchers Richard Wetherill and Charles Mason, searching for their cattle in 1888, are credited with discovering what is now called Cliff

© National Park Service

Ancient National Treasure
Mesa Verde

★★★★★★★★

Palace and Spruce Tree House, the best preserved of the cliff homes. On September 29, 1906, Mesa Verde National Park was created by Congress. Excavation and repair of major sites within the park began two years later.

Covering just over 52,000 acres, Mesa Verde ("green table" in Spanish) holds 4,000 known archaeological sites, including 600 cliff dwellings, as well as mesa-top pit houses (evolved from former storage pits) and pueblos (flat-roofed sandstone, or dried-mud houses with several stories). Some of the dwellings could be quite large: Spruce Tree House, for example, contains 131 rooms and 8 ceremonial chambers built into a natural cave. Puebloans shaped the sandstone blocks for the houses themselves. They filled the space between the blocks with a homemade mortar of soil, water and ash, adding tiny "chinking" stones to make the walls more stable.

Native American Architecture

Native Americans built homes to suit their environment and culture with materials available. Nomadic Plains tribes adopted buffalo skins spread over lean-to timber frames to build highly mobile tepees. Farming tribes of the lower Great Plains, like the Mandans and Pawnees, built permanent earthen lodges. Northwestern tribes erected sturdy plank houses, while the people of the Great Basin and California lowlands preferred light summer lean-tos of thatch and brush, using more substantial materials in winter. Most of the farming people of the Southwest built fixed houses. Like those at Mesa Verde National Park, ancient cliff dwellings and pueblos still stand throughout the region. Latecomers to the Southwest, such as the Navajo, erected six-sided houses called hogans. The probable descendants of the cliff dwellers live today in pueblos. Some, such as the ones in Taos, New Mexico, are stacked like apartment houses and are among the most remarkable buildings in America.

Address: US-160, 10 miles east of Cortez

Phone: 970-529-4465

www.nps.gov/meve

Monticello — © Virginia Tourism Corporation/ Jack Hollingsworth

Charlottesville, Virginia

Set on a hilltop at the center of a 5,000-acre plantation, about two miles southeast of the city of Charlottesville, the house that Thomas Jefferson referred to as his "essay in architecture" stands as an enduring monument to the guiding spirit of the birth of America. Built and rebuilt over a period of 40 years, Jefferson's beloved home captures the talents, broad interests and practicality of the nation's third president. So significant is Monticello that today it is the only house in the U.S. to be included on the UNESCO World Heritage List of international treasures.

Essay in Architecture
Monticello

Defining Moments: 1768

Jefferson began constructing his house on the Little Mountain ("Monticello" in Old Italian) in Virginia's Piedmont region in 1768, the year he was elected to the Virginia House of Burgesses. He based his designs for the original eight-room house on the buildings of ancient Rome, rejecting the symmetrical Georgian architecture so popular at the time.

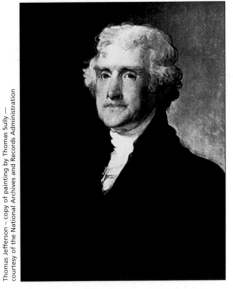

Thomas Jefferson – copy of painting by Thomas Sully – courtesy of the National Archives and Records Administration

Beginning in 1784, Jefferson spent five years in France as trade commissioner and minister. He returned in 1789, and after serving as secretary of State, took a sabbatical to redesign Monticello. Armed with new ideas from his years abroad, Jefferson had the upper story removed and added 21 rooms and the famous dome—the first built on an American house. By the time Jefferson retired from public life in 1809 at the end of his second term as president, the remodeling was nearly completed.

"...all my wishes end where I hope my days will end, at Monticello."

Thomas Jefferson

Although he stated that slavery was an "abominable crime," Jefferson relied heavily on the labor of inherited slaves to run his plantation. The man who drafted legislation to prohibit the importation of slaves into Virginia ironically freed only seven slaves in his lifetime.

On July 4 1826, exactly 50 years after his Declaration of Independence was adopted, Thomas Jefferson died. He is buried on the grounds of Monticello.

A Renaissance Man

Intellectual, philosopher and statesman, Jefferson dabbled in everything from architecture to astronomy. His thoughtful innovations and adaptions are evident at every turn in Monticello, from heat-conserving double doors to skylights to the Great Clock in the entrance hall. Jefferson designed this remarkable timepiece to tell the day and time; it is driven by two sets of weights that resemble small cannonballs. He personally selected all of Monticello's contents, hauling 86 crates of goods home from France and even designing his own furniture. Monticello's expansive grounds became a living laboratory for their owner's experiments in horticulture. Orchards and vegetable gardens flourished here, along with a vineyard and 160 species of trees.

Despite his many accomplishments, Jefferson wanted to be known for only three: as the author of the Declaration of Independence, as the author of the Statute of Virginia for Religious Freedom, and as the Father of the University of Virginia (in Charlottesville). His gravestone, located at Monticello, is inscribed with these achievements.

DRAFTING THE DECLARATION OF INDEPENDENCE.
THE COMMITTEE—FRANKLIN, JEFFERSON, ADAMS, LIVINGSTON AND SHERMAN.

Drafting the Declaration of Independence. The Committee-Franklin, Jefferson, Adams, Livingston and Sherman. Copy of engraving after Alonzo Chappel., 1776. — courtesy of the National Archives and Records Administration

Declaration of Independence — courtesy of the National Archives and Records Administration

Address: On Route 53, east of Route 20

Phone: 434-984-9822

www.monticello.org

Morristown NHP — © National Park Service

Morristown, New Jersey

Morristown is remembered as the site of General Washington's winter encampment, not once, but twice during the Revolutionary War. During the winter of 1777 and the winter of 1780, Washington set about rebuilding his tattered forces, which had shrunk significantly due to desertions and expired enlistments. Disease, chronic supply shortages and severe snowstorms imposed tremendous hardships on the troops, but the Continental army survived. Today Morristown National Historical Park preserves several sites relating to the two grueling winters that Washington and his army endured in the area.

Defining Moments: 1777 and 1780

In early January 1777, following its victory on January 3 in Princeton, the Continental army chose to billet around Morristown, whose strategic location overlooking New York City allowed Washington's men to keep an eye on British forces there. Situated in northern New Jersey's iron-rich hills, the town was also close to munitions manufacturing, an advantage to a commander needing to replenish and re-arm his soldiers.

A more daunting enemy than the British that year was the threat of smallpox. Washington ordered doctors to battle it with a crude inoculation that induced a mild form of the disease to create immunity, a dangerous and much feared procedure. It worked, however, and his men survived. By spring, Washington's army was greatly reinforced. In summer he and his troops left the area in pursuit of the British.

Returning to Morristown in late 1779, the army faced one of the cruelest winters of the 18th century. A deep freeze settled over the land and 26 snowstorms smothered the countryside. Supply lines failed, food sources disappeared and clothing wore thin. Because the Continental Congress was unable to provision his men, Washington appealed to the governors of New Jersey and surrounding states, who, in the general's words, "saved the army." Severely tested, Washington's troops survived nonetheless with a miraculous loss of only 86 men out of some 12,000.

"...the sufferings of the poor soldiers can scarcely be described. While on duty they are unavoidably exposed to all the inclemency of storms and severe cold."

Army surgeon Dr. James Thacher, January 1780

Established in 1933, Morristown National Historical Park includes Fort Nonsense (named for the rumor that its construction was a make-work project), Washington's headquarters at Ford Mansion, and Wick House, headquarters of General St. Clair. Five miles southwest of the town at Jockey Hollow, 10 infantry brigades logged the thick woods to build 1,000 huts as meager protection for 12,000 soldiers during six bitter months of 1779–1780. Though none of the huts survive today, the site quietly evokes the harsh conditions of that difficult winter.

Address: 30 Washington Place

Phone: 973-539-2016

www.nps.gov/morr

Mount Rushmore National Memorial — © National Park Service

Keystone, South Dakota

Looming 6,000 feet above the Great Plains, the massive 60-foot-high granite faces of U.S. presidents George Washington, Thomas Jefferson, Theodore Roosevelt and Abraham Lincoln are carved into South Dakota's Black Hills. These faces now form Mount Rushmore National Memorial, sculptor Gutzon Borglum's "shrine to democracy." His monumental work recognizes the country's greatest leaders and its first 150 years of growth.

Defining Moments: 1927

Armed with ambition, American-born sculptor Gutzon Borglum (1867–1941) arrived in the Black Hills in 1927. He had been invited by South Dakota's state historian, who was impressed by Borglum's sculpture of Robert E. Lee on Stone Mountain in Georgia. President Calvin Coolidge officially sanctioned the monument in August of that year, when he presented the sculptor with six drill bits to begin his work.

Borglum chose Washington, the first U.S. president and commander of the Revolutionary army, as the symbol of the nation's founding. Jefferson, as author of the Declaration of Independence, represents the nation's philosophy and values. Lincoln, whose Civil War leadership restored the Union and ended slavery in the U.S., signifies the country's preservation and progress. Embodying national expansion and guardianship is Theodore Roosevelt, whose progressive stance led to key reforms in conservation, business and world trade.

"... The carving of a mountain, the taking of its several monoliths, pulling them together and making things of them. It is a man's job. It follows me wherever I go and whatever I do."

Gutzon Borglum

Work began in 1927, with funds from the federal government. Borglum and his corps of workers—mostly South Dakota miners—blasted away layers of granite using dynamite and 85-pound pneumatic drills (the actual sculpturing took six and a half years).

During Borglum's absences to seek funding or other commissions, he left his assistants, including his son Lincoln, in charge. After his father died in 1941, Lincoln Borglum added finishing touches, but left the sculpture largely in the stage of completion attained by his father. Mount Rushmore National Memorial was dedicated by President George Bush in July 1991—50 years after Gutzon Borglum's death.

A Monumental Feat

★ Sculptor Gutzon Borglum worked from a scale model he constructed. One inch on the model equalled one foot on the mountain.

★ Over the years, 350 men worked on the monument, usually 35 at a time.

★ During the course of the sculpting, 450,000 tons of rock were removed from the mountain.

★ The total cost of the project, which Borglum originally estimated at $500,000, reached $989,992.

★ On the mountain, George Washington's nose is 20 feet long; Theodore Roosevelt's mustache measures 20 feet across; and Thomas Jefferson's mouth is 18 feet wide.

Address: Route 244, 3 miles west of Keystone

Phone: 605-574-2523

www.nps.gov/moru

Cherished Sanctuary
Mount Vernon

Mount Vernon – west front of mansion
© Mount Vernon Ladies' Association

Alexandria, Virginia

George Washington's beloved home for more than 45 years, Mount Vernon sits on a grassy slope overlooking the Potomac River. It was to this secluded plantation that Washington came to escape the rigors of public service, spend time with his family and live the life of a gentleman farmer. Today, restored to its 1799 appearance, the historic house and remaining 500 acres attract, each year, over one million visitors who come to see the room where Washington dined, the bedchamber where he died and the place where he is buried.

*"I can truly say I would rather be at home at Mount Vernon
with a friend or two about me, than to be attended
the seat of the government by the officers of State
and the representatives of every power in Europe."*

George Washington

Defining Moments: 1761

In 1752, at age 20, Washington took over the management of the 2,500-acre estate, later inheriting it from his half-brother's widow upon her death in 1761. In 1759, after having distinguished himself in the French and Indian War, Washington married Martha Custis, a young widow with two children. Over time he enlarged the property's 1.5-story farmhouse for his family, adding another full story. During his tenure, the estate grew to over 8,000 acres.

George Washington —
© National Archives and Records Administration

He is buried, along with his wife, on the grounds of the property. Not far from his tomb, the slave burial ground holds a memorial to the men and women who worked and sacrificed to make the plantation productive.

Mount Vernon - upper garden
© Mount Vernon Ladies' Association

28 Cherished Sanctuary
Mount Vernon

★★★★★★★★

Plantation Life

Returning home from the Revolution, General Washington set about restoring his farms and finances, which had suffered during the War of Independence (1775–1783). For the next six years, he devoted himself to farming, experimenting with crop rotation and introducing new plant varieties. Washington considered farming the "most delectable" of occupations. Interrupted by his duties as a statesman and an endless stream of visitors—many without invitation—Washington's life at Mount Vernon was, nonetheless, an industrious and satisfying one. Six days a week, he rose early to oversee his operations, which included raising wheat and tobacco, breeding cattle and horses, and cultivating peach and apple orchards. Leisure time was spent fox hunting, fishing, playing cards and billiards, and entertaining prominent Virginians. The man whom Revolutionary officer Henry Lee—Robert E. Lee's father—described as "first in war, first in peace, and first in the hearts of his countrymen," died at Mount Vernon on December 14, 1799, at age 67.

Mount Vernon at Sunrise – photo by Mark Downey © Virginia Tourism Corporation

Address: George Washington Parkway, 8 miles south of Alexandria

Phone: 703-780-2000

www.mountvernon.org

Washington, D.C.

Set back just off the Mall, a massive, Classical-styled rectangular building designed by John Russell Pope holds the treasures of the nation. Inside, a sweeping staircase leads up to the entrance of the National Archives' rotunda. Popularly known as "the Shrine," the cavernous, 75 foot-high domed space inspires reverence. Its centerpiece is an altarlike marble platform where the country's most revered documents are permanently enshrined. On view to the public are the Charters of Freedom—original documents relating to the nation's founding: the Declaration of Independence, all four pages of the Constitution, and the Bill of Rights. The fragile parchments are sealed in specially designed argon-filled cases of titanium and aluminum.

Defining Moments: 1937

Completed in 1937, the National Archives filled a pressing need for a central repository of official and historical records. Before its creation, each department of the federal government stored its own archival material. Important documents were frequently lost or damaged due to haphazard treatment. In 1921, for example, a fire destroyed all of the 1890 census records. That loss, coupled with the Public Building Act of 1926, finally prompted plans to construct a fireproof federal archives building. Today the National Archives and Records Administration, as it is officially designated, safeguards 5 billion paper documents, 9 million aerial photographs, 6 million still photographs and 300,000 video, film and sound recordings.

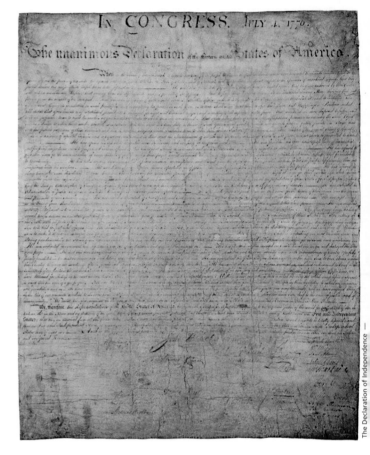

The Declaration of Independence —

Research Facilities

The National Archives functions as a major source of historical material for researchers from the U.S. and abroad. The Central Research Room on the second floor is open to visitors who are undertaking scholarly research. Among the holdings are the papers of the Continental Congress, court and congressional records, historic correspondence and records of federal agencies deemed to be of "enduring value." The Microfilm Research Room on the 4th floor serves persons trying to trace family histories. It contains such materials as the census, military service and pension records and ship-passenger arrival lists.

©National Archives and Records Administration

Mathew Brady photograph of Gen. Ulysses S. Grant and staff of eight ca.1860 - ca.1865
© National Archives and Records Administration

1912 United States Immigration Ship Manifest - © National Archives and Records Administration

A Sampling of Treasures in the Archives

★ 1297 version of England's Magna Carta (a written record of rights demanded of King John by barons at Runnymeade in 1215)

★ George Washington's account book as commander in chief of the Continental army, 1775–1783

★ Continental currency: two-dollar bill printed in 1775, three-dollar bill printed in 1776, 35-dollar bill printed in 1779

★ Commodore Matthew Perry's journals from his historic 19th-century mission to Japan

★ Civil War photographs by Mathew Brady

★ Photo albums of Adolph Hitler's mistress, Eva Braun

Address: Pennsylvania Avenue between 7th and 9th Streets

Phone: 866-272-6272

www.archives.gov

Oklahoma City, Oklahoma

Standing today as a solemn reminder of the April 19, 1995 terrorist bombing of the Murrah Federal Building—the largest terrorist attack on U.S. soil prior to the September 11, 2001 attack on New York City's World Trade Center—the Oklahoma City National Memorial is playing a significant role in the recovery process. Opened in 2000, the memorial commemorates, both individually and collectively, the lives of the 168 men, women and children killed in the explosion. Its three main components are the Outdoor Symbolic Memorial, the Memorial Center Museum, and the Oklahoma City National Memorial Institute for the Prevention of Terrorism.

Defining Moments: 1995

Capital of the state and one of the largest cities, geographically, in the U.S., Oklahoma City sits on the banks of the North Canadian River. In 1993 residents approved over $300 million for urban revitalization. Two years later, the city and the nation were shocked when the Alfred P. Murrah Federal Building was bombed, killing 168 people. To finance a memorial to the victims, the private sector donated $10 million, which was combined with $5 million each from state and federal funds.

Dedicated April 19, 2000—the fifth anniversary of the bombing—the memorial, occupying the site where the Murrah Building stood, was built around a "Survivor Tree" that withstood the explosion. Massive twin gates—the Gates of Time—at each end of a serene reflecting pool are etched with the times immediately before and after the deadly morning blast: 9:01 and 9:03. Placed in 9 rows (for the Murrah building's 9 floors), 168 bronze-backed chairs symbolize the absence and emptiness felt by relatives and friends. The memorial was designed by Hans and Torrey Butzer and Sven Berg, whose submission was chosen from 624 entries in an international competition.

Chairs, Oklahoma City National Memorial — © John G. Anderson/ MICHELIN

"We come here to remember those who were killed, those who survive, and those changed forever. May all who leave here know the impact of violence. May this memorial offer comfort, strength, peace, hope and serenity."

Inscription on the Gates of Time

The Memorial Center, an interactive museum, occupies the adjacent Journal Record Building, also damaged in the incident. Poignant exhibits trace the tragedy and its aftermath, including rescue efforts, world reaction, and prosecution of the crime. The 30,000-square-foot center was opened in February 2001.

Conceived as a living memorial, the Oklahoma City National Memorial Institute for the Prevention of Terrorism was established to reduce and prevent terrorism in other cities. The National Park Service and the Oklahoma City National Memorial Trust operate the memorial in partnership.

Address: 620 N. Harvey Avenue at N.W. 5th Street

Phone: 405-235-3313

www.oklahomacitynationalmemorial.org

Emblem of Infamy
Pearl Harbor

USS Arizona Memorial — © Oahu Visitors Bureau

Honolulu, Hawaii

Few war memorials are as poignant as the USS Arizona Memorial. Floating over the hulk of the sunken battleship, a 184-foot structure marks the permanent tomb of 1,177 crew members killed in the surprise Japanese attack December 7, 1941, on the U.S. naval fleet anchored in Pearl Harbor. In total, more than 2,300 servicemen died and 12 ships, including 6 battleships and 3 destroyers, sank in the nation's greatest military disaster. President Franklin Roosevelt declared it "a date which will live in infamy." The horrific event galvanized the American people—formerly divided over entry into World War II—into actions that ultimately led to the defeat of Japan and the Axis powers.

Defining Moments: 1941

Hawaii's most populated island, Oahu is home to the state capital of Honolulu (Hawaii became the 50th U.S. state in 1959) and to Pearl Harbor, a deep recess in the south-central coast that has served as headquarters of the U.S. Pacific Fleet for nearly 100 years. In November of 1941, a Japanese armada of 33 warships and auxiliary craft headed toward Hawaii. Some 230 miles north of Oahu, Japan launched more than 350 bomber, fighter and torpedo planes on December 7. The attack culminated 10 years of friction between the U.S. and Japan over the empire's increasing expansionism. Protesting Japan's 1937 invasion of China and its 1940 alliance with Germany and Italy, the U.S. froze Japan's U.S. assets and placed an embargo on oil shipments. In July 1941, the

December 7, 1941 Japanese Attack Pearl Harbor — courtesy of the National Archives and Records Administration

U.S. severed financial and commercial relations with Japan. Both governments, however, were in negotiations with each other up until the day of the attack.

"Yesterday, December 7, 1941, a date which will live in infamy, the United States of America was suddenly and deliberately attacked by naval and air forces of the Empire of Japan."

President Franklin D. Roosevelt's Message to Congress, December 8, 1941

Japan believed that its conquest of Southeast Asia and the Western Pacific depended upon eliminating the U.S. fleet. The attack was not a total success: the fleet was shattered, but its aircraft had been away from port on December 7, and the submarine base and storage areas were only slightly damaged. The toll on military personnel, however, was catastrophic: in addition to those killed, 1,178 were wounded.

Ideas for a memorial surfaced in 1943. With public and private funds, the USS Arizona Memorial was completed in 1961 and dedicated the following year. The National Park Service took over its administration in 1980. Annually, more than one million people, many of whom are from Japan, visit the site.

Address: 1 Arizona Memorial Drive

Phone: 808-422-0561

www.nps.gov/usar

Bastion of Military Might
The Pentagon

★★★★★★★★

The Pentagon — Master Sgt. Ken Hammond, U.S. Air Force

Arlington, Virginia

The heart of the American military establishment, this huge five-sided building houses the offices of the highest authorities within America's armed services—the secretary of Defense and the Joint Chiefs of Staff (Army, Navy, Air Force and Marines)—all of whom answer to the commander in chief, the president of the U.S. One of the world's largest single-structure office buildings, the Pentagon contains six-and-a-half-million square feet. Each of its five sides is larger than the Capitol building; together they contain just over 17 miles of corridors.

Defining Moments: 1943

Army engineers were given one weekend in July 1941 to design the building, which was to be situated on the Arlington shore of the Potomac River. Since the lot was five-sided, they devised a pentagonal shape. Built of reinforced concrete faced with limestone, the 5-story Pentagon was completed in 16 months on January 15, 1943. On September 11, 2001, its west wall was struck by a hijacked commercial airliner, resulting in the loss of 189 lives.

Address: I-395 at Washington Boulevard

Phone: 703-697-1776

www.defenselink.mil/pubs/pentagon

Manitou Springs, Colorado

At 14,110 feet elevation, Pikes Peak is probably the most famous apex in America, though not the highest. Located 10 miles west of Colorado Springs, the peak is known for its accessibility and unrivaled views—extending west into the snow-capped Rockies, east across the Great Plains, north to Denver and south to the Sangre de Cristo Range. The magnificent panorama Katharine Lee Bates beheld from the summit in 1893 inspired her to write the poem that would become the lyrics to "America the Beautiful," a much-loved national song.

Defining Moments: 1806

In 1806 Army Lieutenant Zebulon Pike declared the mountain "unconquerable" after his expeditionary party was thwarted in their attempt to climb it. Successfully scaled in 1820, the mountain was a magnet for fortune seekers by 1859 when gold found in the area spawned the slogan "Pikes Peak or Bust." Today ascent is possible by foot, by vehicle or by the popular cog railway.

Pikes Peak seen from the Garden of the Gods, Colorado —
© The Colorado Springs Convention and Visitors Bureau

Address: Cog Railway at 515 Ruxton Avenue

Phone: 719-385-7325

www.pikespeakcolorado.com

34 Symbol of a New Beginning
Plymouth Rock

Plymouth Rock Enclosure © PhotoDisc

Plymouth, Massachusetts

Regarded traditionally as the stepping stone used by the Mayflower passengers when they disembarked at Plymouth in 1620, Plymouth Rock has come to symbolize a fresh start, leaving the old for the new. Set at harbor's edge, facing Cape Cod Bay, the boulder is protected by a columned granite enclosure. Resembling a Greek temple, the structure serves as a modern-day shrine to the fortitude of these early colonists, who, along with their helpful Native American neighbors, celebrated the now time-honored tradition of Thanksgiving.

Defining Moments: 1620

Toward the end of the 16th century, a group of English Puritans known as Separatists attempted to reform the Church of England by breaking away from it. In 1607, to avoid persecution by the authorities, members of the group emigrated from Scrooby, England, to Holland. They remained there until, impressed by favorable accounts of

the New World, they decided to emigrate to America. Early in September 1620, 102 passengers, including 35 Separatists, boarded the Mayflower at Plymouth, England, and set sail for the Virginia Colony in North America. Their ship landed two months later, however, on the shores of Cape Cod. They spent five weeks in the region before again setting sail. Perhaps detoured by strong winds, they headed for the bay that had been charted six years earlier by Captain John Smith, an English explorer who had helped establish Jamestown, Virginia, in 1607. It was on the shores of Cape Cod Bay that the Pilgrims, as they have become known, founded Plymouth Colony.

"To think of landing here [at Plymouth] on the 22nd of December without a shelter and 3,000 miles from what once was a beloved home. The idea as I stood upon the burying place which...overlooks the harbour made me shiver."

Charles Francis Adams, Diary, 14 September 1835

Harsh weather and a scarcity of food left almost half the colony dead by the end of the first winter. Spring brought hope to the settlement, along with a group of Native Americans who befriended the Pilgrims and taught them how to hunt, fish, and raise crops. After the harvest that fall, members of Plymouth Colony joined with the Indians in a three-day feast in gratitude for their blessings.

Pilgrims and Puritans

Not until 200 years after their arrival in Plymouth, when William Bradford's journal was discovered, did the colonists become known as Pilgrims. In it, the Separatist leader of the Mayflower expedition referred to the passengers who left Holland as "pilgrimes." The Separatists were a radical faction of Puritanism, a movement begun in the late-16th century intent on purifying the Church of England of Roman Catholic influence.

Address: Water Street

Phone: 800-872-1620

www.visit-plymouth.com

Arlington House, Robert E. Lee Memorial — Courtesy of Arlington House, NPS

Arlington, Virginia

Surrounded by Arlington Cemetery, the former home of Robert E. Lee, hero of the Confederacy, tops a high bluff overlooking Washington, D.C. Though military postings often placed him elsewhere, Lee considered Arlington House his true home. Six of his seven children were born in the mansion, and it was in his bedchamber that Lee drafted his resignation from the Union army. Today Arlington House, as the Robert E. Lee Memorial is commonly known, stands as a tribute to the widely respected Civil War general who defended the South.

Defining Moments: 1861

After Lee married Mary Custis in 1831, they took up residence in Arlington House, her father's 1817 mansion set on a 1,100-acre tract across the Potomac River from the new federal city. For 30 years, Arlington House was home to the couple, despite frequent military travel. In April 1861, Lee left for Richmond, where he accepted command of the Army of Northern Virginia. He would never again return to his beloved home. A month later, Union troops made Arlington House the headquarters for the Army of the Potomac and in 1864 the grounds were turned into a cemetery for Civil War dead. In 1925 Congress designated the house a national memorial.

"My affections and attachments are more strongly placed [at Arlington House] than at any other place in the world."

Robert E. Lee

Portrait of a Great American

Robert Edward Lee was born in Stratford, Virginia on January 19, 1807, the fourth child of Revolutionary War colonel Henry Lee and his wife. Unable to afford college tuition, Lee sought an appointment to the U.S. Military Academy at West Point, where he graduated second in his class in 1829. Two years later, he married and eventually fathered seven children. Over the next 30 years, Lee pursued his military career, distinguishing himself as a leader in the field of battle. When South Carolina seced-

Robert E. Lee — © National Park Service

ed from the Union in 1860, Lee, who opposed war, wrote: "(If) strife and civil war are to take the place of brotherly love and kindness, I shall mourn for my country and for the welfare and progress of mankind." In April 1861 Lee was offered command of the new Union army. Although he was against slavery, Lee refused the post, fearing it might require his leading troops against Southern states, even against his beloved homeland of Virginia. When Virginia voted to secede, Lee resigned his commission from the U.S. Army to help defend his native state. Although Lee proved himself a brilliant general during the Civil War, he was finally beaten back by General Grant's army in 1865 and surrendered at Appomattox Court House, Virginia on April 9. After the war, Lee served as president of a college in Lexington, Virginia, where he died in 1870.

Address: On the grounds of Arlington National Cemetery

Phone: 703-235-1530

www.nps.gov/arho

Bringing Space Down to Earth
Space Center Houston

© Greater Houston Convention and Visitors Bureau

Clear Lake, Texas

Space Center Houston is a place where non-astronauts can try on space helmets, touch moon rocks and "walk" in distant galaxies, among other activities. Located 25 miles south of Houston, it's the official visitors center for the adjacent Johnson Space Center—the National Aeronautics and Space Administration's (NASA) Mission Control, research and astronaut training facility for the U.S. space program. Live shows, guided tours and interactive exhibits at the visitors center allow the public to "experience" space travel and to appreciate the sophisticated missions, such as Gemini and Apollo, that have been developed at the decades-old facility.

Defining Moments: 1961

Established in 1961 as the Manned Spacecraft Center, NASA's facility was renamed in 1973 in honor of Lyndon Johnson, a native of Texas and the country's 36th president. The center's Mission Control has overseen the design and testing of America's manned space flights since the Gemini IV mission in 1965. Home to the nation's astronaut corps, Johnson Space Center uses its high-tech equipment and facilities to prepare flight crews for the Space Shuttle and the International Space Station.

© Greater Houston Convention and Visitors Bureau

America's Space Firsts

★ First U.S. earth satellite, Explorer 1 – January 1958

★ First American in space, Alan B. Shepard. Jr., aboard
　　Freedom 7 – May 1961

★ First American to orbit earth, John Glenn Jr., aboard
　　Mercury – February 1962

★ First American to walk in space, Edward White, outside
　　Gemini 4 – June 1965

★ First manned orbits of the moon: Frank Borman, James Lovell
　　and William Anders, Apollo 8 mission – October 1968

★ First manned moon launch: Apollo 11 mission – July 1969

★ First man to walk on the moon, Neil Armstrong – July 1969

★ First cooperative international space flight: Apollo 18 links
　　with the U.S.S.R.'s Soyuz 19 – July 1975

★ First space shuttle launch from Cape Canaveral – April 12, 1981

Address: 1601 NASA Road, off I-45

Phone: 281-244-2100

www.spacecenter.org

37

The Promise of Freedom
Statue of Liberty

Statue of Liberty at sunset © PhotoDisc

New York, New York

At the entrance to New York harbor, a lone statue of a woman, 151-feet high, with upraised arm holding a torch, has welcomed travelers arriving by sea for more than a century. The seven points in her crown signify liberty radiating out to the seven continents and the seven seas. In her left hand she holds a tablet representing the Declaration of Independence and bearing the date of its proclamation, July 4, 1776. Her right hand grasps the torch, symbolically lighting the world with the promise of freedom and justice for all. A gift from France to the American people, "Miss Liberty" stands as a stirring reminder of the ideals upon which the nation was founded.

Defining Moments: 1886

In 1871 Alsatian sculptor Frédéric-Auguste Bartholdi was selected to design a memorial commemorating the friendship between France and the U.S. (which dates back to the American Revolution). On his voyage to America to gather ideas for the project, he was overwhelmed by the grandeur of the scene before him as his ship entered New York harbor. He knew then that the monument would be a figure of Liberty,

A Few Facts
★★★★★★★

Weight:	225 tons
Height:	151 feet
Height of torch:	305 feet above sea level
Head:	10 feet by 17 feet
Right arm:	42 feet long, 12 feet in diameter
Index finger:	8 feet long

and one of the tiny harbor islands in this breathtaking setting would be the ideal site for it.

The project was to be a joint effort: the French would pay for the statue itself, and the Americans would raise funds for a pedestal. Bartholdi began work on the sculpture in 1874, calling upon French engineer Gustave Eiffel, who later built the Paris tower that bears his name, to create a skeletal steel frame for the 300 copper plates forming Liberty's "skin." By 1884 the statue was finished. It was transported to the U.S. in 1885 to be installed on a pedestal designed by American architect Richard Morris Hunt.

At the dedication ceremony on October 28, 1886, President Grover Cleveland presided over the statue's unveiling, accompanied by a 21-gun salute, bellowing foghorns and the illumination of Liberty's crown, shining as a beacon of hope to the millions who would flock to America's shore.

Statue of Liberty ©Joseph Pobereskin/ NYC & Company, Inc.

"*Give me your tired, your poor,*
Your huddled masses yearning to breathe free,
The wretched refuse of your teeming shore.
Send these, the homeless, tempest-tost to me,
I lift my lamp beside the golden door!"

From a poem by Emma Lazarus
inscribed on the Statue of Liberty's pedestal

Address: Liberty Island

Phone: 212-363-3200

www.nps.gov/stli

Service Before Self
U.S. Air Force Academy

★★★★★★★★

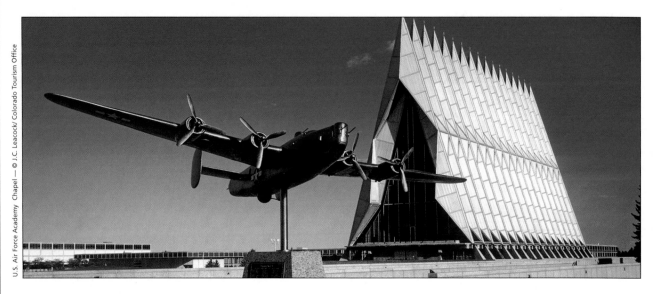

U.S. Air Force Academy Chapel — © J.C. Leacock/ Colorado Tourism Office

Colorado Springs, Colorado

Sprawling over 29 square miles at the foot of the Rampart Range in the Rocky Mountains, this training facility is the only U.S. service academy in the West. Located 12 miles north of downtown Colorado Springs, the institution offers a four-year curriculum leading to a commissioned office in the U.S. Air Force. The 18,000-acre campus houses some 4,000 cadets and is recognizable by its soaring, interfaith chapel topped with 17 aluminum spires, each 150 feet high.

Defining Moments: 1958

Initiated by an act of Congress in 1954, the academy officially opened in 1955 at Lowry Air Force Base in Denver in temporary facilities. The academy moved to its present permanent quarters in late 1958. Candidates, the majority nominated by U.S. senators and representatives, must pass a competitive exam to be admitted. Cadets undertake an aerospace-oriented military program coupled with extensive physical education. Courses include history, geography, physics and aeronautical engineering. Most graduates continue on to Air Force pilot training schools, if they meet the physical requirements.

Address: Academy Drive off I-25 at Exit 156B (North Gate Boulevard)

Phone: 719-333-1110

www.usafa.af.mil

Honor, Courage, Commitment
U.S. Naval Academy

★★★★★★★★

Annapolis, Maryland

Future officers in the U.S. Navy and U.S. Marine Corps study on this peaceful, 338-acre campus bordering the Severn River within the historic port city of Annapolis, founded in 1648. "The Yard," as the academy grounds are called, includes Bancroft Hall, the 1906 Baroque structure in the center of campus that covers 27 acres and contains five miles of corridors. Few buildings in Annapolis rival the copper-domed Navy Chapel modeled after the Hôtel des Invalides in Paris. Some 4,000 men and women are enrolled here in academic and professional courses leading to commissions in the U.S. Navy and the U.S. Marine Corps.

U.S. Naval Academy — © Annapolis & Anne Arundel County CVB

Defining Moments: 1845

The academy was established in 1845 on the shores of Chesapeake Bay. For 85 years, from 1860 to 1945, the majority of officers in the Navy were academy graduates. The Naval Academy serves as the undergraduate college for the U.S. Navy. Midshipmen are enrolled in a four-year program in subjects that include engineering, science, mathematics and the humanities. In summer midshipmen augment their studies by training at naval bases and on fleet ships.

Address: 121 Blake Road

Phone: 410-263-6933

www.nadn.navy.mil

Shuttle © Alabama Bureau of Tourism & Travel/Dan Brothers

Huntsville, Alabama

The U.S. Space and Rocket Center shelters the world's largest collection of spacecraft. Located 99 miles north of Birmingham, the center lies on the perimeter of the U.S. Army's legendary Redstone Arsenal, a 38,000-acre military post just southwest of Huntsville's city center. Since Redstone Arsenal and the Marshall Space Flight Center have restricted access, the state of Alabama opened "the world's largest space-travel attraction" nearby, the most heavily visited tourist destination in Alabama. Home to popular children's space camp programs, the U.S. Space and Rocket Center offers earthlings an outer space experience via interactive gadgetry and complex exhibits.

Defining Moments: 1970

The former mill town of Huntsville changed abruptly during World War II when the U.S. Army created Redstone Arsenal to make chemical weapons. Then, in 1950, the army hired Dr. Wernher von Braun and 117 other German rocket scientists to propel the U.S. into the forefront of space exploration. With the creation of the National Aeronautics and Space Administration (NASA) in 1958, the team of scientists became civilian rather than military employees, and the large research site at Redstone was converted into the Marshall Space Flight Center. Occupying 1,800 acres, this center ranks as the major research and testing arm of the U.S. space-exploration industry.

Opened by the state in 1970, the U.S. Space and Rocket Center provides visitors with the only public access to Marshall Space Flight Center via a narrated bus tour. Tour stops vary according to activities within the NASA compound; recently the staff has focused on the International Space Station, a permanent orbiting scientific laboratory developed by the U.S., Russia, Canada, Japan and the 14 member nations of the European Space Agency.

Shuttle © Huntsville Convention & Visitors Bureau

The center offers several simulated space shuttle rides to Mars, Jupiter, and points beyond; and visitors can also see the actual 1972 Apollo 16 command module and a walk-in module of the tiny quarters of the Russian Mir Space Station. A Skylab mock-up used for astronaut training provides a fascinating glimpse into the realities of long-term space travel—such as how to take a shower when the soap and water float. Outside, the gigantic Saturn V rocket and a full-scale model of the Pathfinder space shuttle, complete with external tank and rocket boosters, are on display.

In the five-day space camp programs for children 9 to 18 years of age, youngsters participate in simulated missions, launches, scientific experiments and other space-related activities.

Space Camp ©Huntsville Convention & Visitors Bureau

Address: One Tranquility Base, off I-565 in Huntsville

Phone: 256-837-3400

www.spacecamp.com

Triumph of the Human Spirit
Valley Forge

© National Park Service

Valley Forge, Pennsylvania

Once the site of iron-forging operations, Valley Forge is synonymous in the minds of many Americans with extreme suffering and sacrifice. It was here, from December 19, 1777, to June 19, 1778, that General George Washington and his under-provisioned, poorly clothed and starving troops camped along the Schuylkill River, enduring a bitterly cold winter. By spring, the extraordinary fortitude and resolve of these men and their leaders had helped shape the ragged Continental army into a professional fighting force that, aided by the French, would ultimately vanquish the British and set the American colonies free. Today, the 3,400-acre Valley Forge National Historic Park commemorates Washington's encampment during the harsh winter of 1777–1778.

Defining Moments: 1777–1778

Exhausted by a grueling autumn campaign, Washington's army marched into Valley Forge in December 1777. Here, close enough to monitor the British troops in Philadelphia, some 20 miles northwest, the poorly provisioned troops hastened to

erect log huts in which to weather the Pennsylvania winter. By late December, a combination of illness, hunger and improper clothing rendered the majority of the Continental soldiers unfit for duty. It was then that General Washington wrote an impassioned letter to Congress on behalf of his neglected forces, who, he said, would be forced to either "starve, dissolve, or disperse" without an infusion of new provisions. The grim situation slowly began to brighten by the end of January, when congressional delegates visited the camp and took measures to increase supplies.

> *"Naked and starving as they are, we cannot enough admire the incomparable patience and fidelity of the soldiery."*
>
> General George Washington, February 16, 1778

In late February, Prussian army veteran Baron Friedrich Wilhelm von Steuben arrived at Valley Forge from France. Offering his military expertise to General Washington, he was appointed Acting Inspector General responsible for training. In unconventional fashion, he worked directly with the soldiers, rigorously drilling the poorly trained Continental troops in Prussian military techniques. He is largely credited with imposing order and precision on the men, teaching them to march in disciplined columns, load muskets with efficiency and charge effectively with bayonets. By spring the formerly dispirited army was better disciplined and reinvigorated with both new recruits and the news that France would support the Patriots' cause.

Today the national park contains the remains of earthworks and the 1760s fieldstone house that served as Washington's headquarters, as well as cannons, reconstructed log huts and the monumental National Memorial Arch honoring the men who wintered here during a severe testing time in the Revolutionary War.

Address: North Gulph Road

Phone: 610-783-1077

www.nps.gov/vafo

Key to War's End
Vicksburg

Vicksburg National Military Park — © Mississippi Development Authority/ Division of Tourism

Vicksburg, Mississippi

Dominating a 200-foot bluff overlooking the mighty Mississippi River, Vicksburg was a strategic fortress and critical Confederate port, whose fall signaled a turning point in the Civil War. Besieged for 47 days, Vicksburg finally surrendered on July 4, 1863, giving the North control of the "Father of Waters" and dividing the Confederacy in two from north to south. Today Vicksburg National Military Park preserves the 1,800-acre battleground, marked by reconstructed earthworks, emplaced cannon, 1,325 monuments to the various state regiments, and a restored Union gunboat. Also part of the park, Vicksburg National Cemetery contains the graves of 17,000 Union soldiers as well as those of veterans from subsequent wars. Confederate dead were buried in Vicksburg City Cemetery.

Defining Moments: 1863

The Mississippi River was essential to the movement of Union troops and supplies into the South. To guard this vital waterway, the Confederates had built forts along it at strategic locations. By mid-1862, Union troops had captured all of these outposts except Port Hudson (in Louisiana) and Vicksburg—the more important of the two. Called "the Gibraltar of the Confederacy," Vicksburg was so strategically situated that it took Union commanders Ulysses S. Grant and William T. Sherman more than a year of planning, tunnel-digging and fierce fighting to capture the city in July 1863.

> *"See what a lot of land these fellows hold, of which Vicksburg is the key. The war can never be brought to a close until that key is in our pocket."*

President Abraham Lincoln

At first, however, General Grant sought a quick victory at Vicksburg. Of Grant's 45,000 troops, only General Sherman's corps was well positioned to attack the city. Initial Union assaults, on May 19 and 22, 1863, were repulsed, though, by Vicksburg's defenders. Grant then ordered a formal siege: Union forces planted charges in tunnels they had carved under enemy lines, set up artillery to pound Confederate fortifications, and positioned 60 gunboats to bombard the city from the river. By late June, Lieutenant General John Pemberton, in command of the Confederate forces, knew the Union's cordon could not be broken. On July 4, 1863, he accepted Grant's terms of surrender. Five days later, Port Hudson surrendered: the Mississippi River, under Confederate control since the war's beginning, was finally free of Southern domination.

Address: US-61/80 (Clay Street), just west of I-20

Phone: 601-636-0583

www.nps.gov/vick

National Heroes/Fallen Heroes
War Memorials

Washington, D.C. Area

Each a unique portrayal of the heroic actions and monumental sacrifices of U.S. armed forces and auxiliary personnel, four poignant memorials pay tribute to the men and women who served this country, especially during wartime. Across the Potomac River, in Arlington, Virginia, the Marine Corps War Memorial honors all U.S. Marines who lost their lives in military duty. On the Mall in Washington, D.C., the Korean War Veterans Memorial, the Vietnam Veterans Memorial and the World War II Memorial commemorate the service personnel of three international conflicts.

★ Marine Corps War Memorial (Iwo Jima Memorial)

On February 19, 1945, U.S. Marines landed on the Japanese-held island of Iwo Jima, initiating one of the deadliest battles of World War II. In 36 days of fighting, the U.S. lost more than 6,500 soldiers. The capture of this strategically located island is considered one of the Marines' greatest victories in the American campaign in the Pacific.

The six sculpted figures of the famed memorial, which was dedicated in 1954 in Arlington, Virginia, depict Americans in combat uniform struggling to raise the Stars and Stripes above Mount Suribachi. Horace W. Peaslee's design was based on James Rosenthal's Pulitzer Prize-winning photograph. Felix de Weldon sculptured the stirring scene.

Marine Corps War Memorial © PhotoDisc

Korean War Memorial —
© Washington, DC Convention and Tourism Corporation

★ Korean War Veterans Memorial

North Korea's invasion of South Korea on June 25, 1950, prompted President Harry S Truman to deploy U.S. troops in an attempt to prevent the Communist North from overrunning the U.S.-supported South. After three years of combat, an armistice was signed on July 27, 1953. Of the 1.5 million Americans involved, more than 54,000 died, over 110,000 were captured or wounded and some 8,000 were declared missing.

Located southeast of the Lincoln Memorial, this compelling ensemble of statues, freestanding wall and circular pool honors the members of the U.S. armed forces who served in the Korean War. Nineteen seven-foot-high stainless-steel statues of men in patrol formation immediately identify the memorial, which was dedicated in 1995. To one side, a wall of polished black granite is etched with the faces of some 2,500 servicemen and servicewomen. Other components bear the statistics of the war's casualties and those missing in action as well as the words: "Freedom is not Free."

Vietnam Veterans Memorial © PhotoDisc

★ Vietnam Veterans Memorial

Large-scale military action in Vietnam began in 1965 when the first battle took place between the Americans and North Vietnamese in the La Drang Valley. U.S. troops would continue to engage in combat until the cease-fire of January 1973 signed in Paris. Not until 1975, as Communist forces moved on Saigon, did President Gerald Ford announce that U.S. involvement in Vietnam had ended.

Inset in a low hill, designer Maya Lin's compelling memorial, which was completed in 1982, is actually two triangular walls that join at a 125-degree angle. Composed of black granite from India, they hold the names of the more than 58,000 men and women killed, imprisoned or missing. Commonly called the Wall, Lin's work was conceived as a symbol of healing. It has become the moving shrine it was intended to be, a place where family and friends can touch the names of loved ones lost in battle.

National World War II Memorial —
© Washington, DC Convention and Tourism Corporation

★ National World War II Memorial

The Second World War (1939–45) was fought on all but one of the seven continents and involved most of the world's powerful nations. Some 50 million people were killed, millions wounded and millions left homeless. In this global conflict, the Axis powers of Germany, Italy and Japan confronted the Allied Forces of Great Britain, France, the Soviet Union, China and a number of smaller nations, joined in 1941 by the United States. By September 1945, the last surrender was signed; the Allies were finally victorious.

Located near the Reflecting Pool on the east-west axis between the Lincoln Memorial and the Washington Monument, the National World War II Memorial was dedicated on Memorial Day 2004. Architect Friedrich St. Florian's design includes identical arched pavilions, which symbolize the Atlantic and Pacific theaters of the war. Each bearing a bronze wreath, 56 pillars representing U.S. states and territories line the ends of the plaza. Backdropped by the Reflecting Pool, a Freedom Wall bears 4,000 gold stars, each star symbolic of 100 American war-related deaths.

Address: N. Meade Street, Arlington and The Mall at 21st Street N.W. & 17th Street N.W.

Phone: 202-426-6841

www.nps.gov/nacc

Washington Monument — © Jake McGuire / Washington, DC Convention and Tourism Corporation

Washington, D.C.

The capital's most conspicuous landmark, and the world's tallest freestanding stone structure, this austere marble obelisk rises 555 feet from a knoll in the middle of the Mall. Though it took nearly four decades to complete, the monument, ringed by U.S. flags, stands as a commanding memorial to the man who was "Father of the Nation" and as an indelible symbol of the city that bears his name. Soldier, farmer and public servant, Washington was a rock of strength and resolve as head of the Continental army and a wellspring of vision and restraint as the first president of the United States.

Defining Moments: 1888

In 1783 the Continental Congress passed a resolution to erect a statue honoring the hero of the Revolution. Lack of funds delayed the project for decades. Eventually, a group of citizens raised $28,000 by 1836 in a public drive, and architect Robert Mills was chosen to design a "grand circular colonnaded building...from which springs an

obelisk shaft." Progress was slow due to insufficient funding. After 12 years, the corner-stone was laid on July 4, 1848. Work ceased when the funds ran dry in 1853. Finally, after nearly 25 years, an act of Congress authorized the government to complete the project. Dedicated on February 21, 1885, the monument opened to the public in 1888.

Father of the Nation

In 1789 the new electoral college unanimously voted Washington the first president of the nation. Faced with defining the presidency, Washington proceeded cautiously. He managed to keep the young country out of European wars, and to establish federal authority over individual states and presidential authority over issues of foreign policy. He argued (unsuccessfully) against the adoption of a partisan political system. He also approved the construction of the new federal city that would bear his name. After eight years and two terms as president, he refused a third and in 1797 retired for a final time to Mount Vernon.

Military Commander

George Washington (1732–1799) began his long service to this country while in his early 20s, distinguishing himself as a commander during the French and Indian War in the 1750s. In 1775, at the Second Continental Congress, he was unanimously elected head of the Continental army. For eight years Washington spearheaded the fight against Britain, frequently keeping the war effort alive through the strength of his own convictions. In addition to battling the superior forces of the British, Washington had to contend with his own poorly trained, often unenthusiastic troops, as well as with a fickle Congress reluctant to provide funds or moral support. After countless set-backs and lost battles, the Continentals, thanks to Washington's military brilliance and the help of French allies, won a decisive victory against Lord Cornwallis' troops on October 19, 1781, at Yorktown, Virginia.

Address: The Mall at 15th Street N.W.

Phone: 202-426-6841

www.nps.gov/nacc

45

Duty, Honor, Country
West Point

Color Guard, West Point — © West Point

West Point, New York

Overlooking the Hudson River, some 50 miles north of New York City, West Point is renowned as the site of the United States Military Academy. The oldest of the nation's service academies, it was founded in 1802 by an act of Congress, signed by President Jefferson. Today more than 4,000 men and women cadets follow in the footsteps of illustrious graduates, such as generals Douglas MacArthur (1903), George Patton (1909), Dwight Eisenhower (1915) and Norman Schwartzkopf (1956), who served the nation as commanding officers in the U.S. Army. Other celebrated alumni include Civil War generals Robert E. Lee (1829) and Ulysses S. Grant (1843) as well as astronauts Frank Borman (1950), Nelson "Buzz" Aldrin (1951) and Edward White (1952).

Defining Moments: 1802

Fortress West Point was built in 1778 during the War of Independence as a series of fortifications to protect the strategically important Hudson River at this most defensi-

1828 sketch of the Academy — © West Point

ble location. After the war the grounds became a repository for trophies and captured equipment. It was not until March 16, 1802, that the U.S. Military Academy was authorized by Congress as a school for military engineers; in 1812 it was reorganized as a four-year college leading to professional military service.

"Duty, honor, country. These three hallowed words reverently dictate what you ought to be, what you can be, what you will be."

General Douglas MacArthur May 12, 1962

Entering as Fourth Class cadets, today's freshmen (called "plebes") enroll in a curriculum leading to a Bachelor of Science degree. They are constantly watched by the upper classes for possible violation of regulations. Plebes are also subject to inspection around the clock. In preparation for a career as a military officer, cadets train in hand-to-hand combat and mountain warfare, among other courses. Intensive athletics and extracurricular activities round out their studies, which emphasize the development of leadership skills. Cadets are actually members of the U.S. Army and receive a special pay set by Congress, which they use to cover the cost of their uniforms and textbooks.

Photographs of West Point often capture cadets—smartly dressed in uniforms similar to those worn in the War of 1812—marching in precision on the expansive lawn known as The Plain. Adjacent to this parade ground stands Battle Monument, a granite shaft raised to memorialize soldiers killed during the Civil War. Rising over The Plain, at a height of 300 feet, is the Gothic-styled Cadet Chapel (1910), built in the form of a cross. An outdoor museum, Trophy Point features cannons captured in every major American war.

Parade, West Point — © West Point

Among the bronze plaques on campus memorializing Revolutionary and Mexican War combatants, the name of traitor Benedict Arnold, the commanding general at West Point who conspired to betray the fortifications in 1780, has been eradicated.

Address: Thayer Gate, past Highland Falls on Route 9 West

Phone: 845-938-2638

www.usma.edu

The White House © PhotoDisc

Washington, D.C.

Universally recognized symbol of the U.S. presidency, the stately residence at 1600 Pennsylvania Avenue presides over 18 acres of gardens and lawns facing Lafayette Park in the nation's capital. Forty-three U.S. presidents have called this mansion home, beginning with John Adams in 1800. Inside, the ground-floor and first-floor rooms function as formal state reception areas, while the First Family's private living quarters occupy the second and third floors. Welcoming visitors year-round, the White House is reputedly the only president's home in the world that is open to the public.

Defining Moments: 1800

Envisioned by Washington, D.C.'s designer, Pierre L'Enfant, as a grand palatial structure, the White House was ultimately designed by a young Irish builder, James Hoban. It has evolved into its present form over a period of 150 years. L'Enfant left the capital in a huff in 1792, after a series of conflicts with the city commissioners. Suddenly finding themselves without an architectural plan, the commissioners announced a public design competition for the president's house. The $500 prize went to Hoban, whose plan called for a three-story Georgian-style house.

Home to America's Presidents
The White House

Although the building's cornerstone was laid in October 1792, work proceeded slowly due to a shortage of skilled labor and public funds. In 1793 President George Washington agreed to omit the third floor in order to save money, and Hoban redrew plans for a two-story residence. (The third floor was added in 1927.)

> *"May none but Honest and Wise*
> *Men ever rule under This Roof."*

John Adams, in a letter to his wife

Completed too late to house Washington, the White House was finally habitable in 1800, and President John Adams moved into the drafty—and still incomplete—mansion. The first long-term resident (1801–09) of the presidential palace was Thomas Jefferson, who commissioned Benjamin Latrobe to add the colonnaded wings on the east and west sides of the house.

James Madison's stay in the Executive Mansion was marked by disaster. In August 1814, during the War of 1812, the British entered the city and set fire to the White House. Madison's wife, Dolley, is credited with rescuing many important documents and a portrait of George Washington by Gilbert Stuart. Though saved from burning to the ground by a timely summer rain, the mansion had to be completely rebuilt.

The White House —
©Washington, DC Convention and Tourism Corporation

Throughout the 19th century, architectural changes were implemented as funds became available. In 1902 Theodore Roosevelt entrusted the firm of McKim, Mead and White with a large-scale renovation of the White House. Among other things, the architects added the west wing and an expansive carriage porch on the east.

Presidents of the United States

★ ★ ★ ★ ★ ★ ★

George Washington (1789–97)

John Adams (1797–1801)

Thomas Jefferson (1801–09)

James Madison (1809–17)

James Monroe (1817–25)

John Quincy Adams (1825–29)

Andrew Jackson (1829–37)

Martin Van Buren (1837–41)

William Henry Harrison (1841)

John Tyler (1841–45)

James Polk (1845–49)

Zachary Taylor (1849–50)

Millard Fillmore (1850–53)

Franklin Pierce (1853–57)

James Buchanan (1857–61)

Abraham Lincoln (1861–65)

Andrew Johnson (1865–69)

Ulysses S. Grant (1869–77)

Rutherford B. Hayes (1877–81)

James A. Garfield (1881)

Chester A. Arthur (1881–85)

Grover Cleveland (1885–89)

Benjamin Harrison (1889–93)

Grover Cleveland (1893–97)

William McKinley (1897–1901)

Theodore Roosevelt (1901–09)

William Howard Taft (1909–13)

Woodrow Wilson (1913–21)

Warren Harding (1921–23)

Calvin Coolidge (1923–29)

Herbert Hoover (1929–33)

Franklin D. Roosevelt (1933–45)

Harry S Truman (1945–53)

Dwight Eisenhower (1953–61)

John F. Kennedy (1961–63)

Lyndon B. Johnson (1963–69)

Richard Nixon (1969–74)

Gerald Ford (1974–77)

Jimmy Carter (1977–81)

Ronald Reagan (1981–89)

George H. Bush (1989–93)

Bill Clinton (1993–2001)

George W. Bush (2001–)

Address: 1600 Pennsylvania Avenue

Phone: 202-456-1414

www.whitehouse.gov

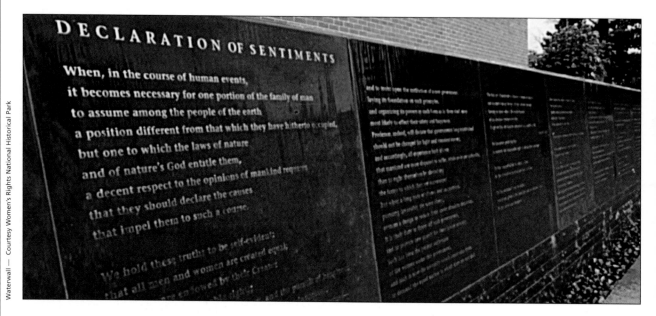

Waterwall — Courtesy Women's Rights National Historical Park

Seneca Falls, New York

Inspired by the growing movement in the 1830s to abolish slavery, a group of women in Seneca Falls determined to extend the spirit of reform to American women, whose legal rights were very limited. Using the powerful language of the Declaration of Independence, they drafted a manifesto of women's rights and in 1848 held the first Women's Rights Convention in a chapel on Seneca Falls' main street. It would be 72 years before the 19th Amendment, guaranteeing women across the nation the right to vote, was officially added to the U.S. Constitution on August 26, 1920. In the interim, several Western states, including Colorado (1893), Idaho and Utah (1896), began granting women the vote. Today the Women's Rights National Historical Park celebrates the convention and those closely associated with the movement, principally Elizabeth Cady Stanton, Susan B. Anthony, Lucretia Mott and Frederick Douglass.

"The right of citizens of the United States to vote shall not be denied or abridged by the United States or by any State on account of sex . . . Congress shall have power to enforce this article by appropriate legislation."

19th Amendment to the U.S. Constitution

Defining Moments: 1848

Lucretia Mott and her husband were involved in the abolitionist movement, providing sanctuary for slaves in their home. Her interest in women's rights surfaced when, as a young teacher, she was paid half the salary the male teachers received. Daughter of a U.S. congressman, Elizabeth Cady Stanton knew how much the country's laws discriminated against women, a wrong she was eager to right. In 1840 in London, at the World's Anti-Slavery Convention—to which Lucretia Mott and Stanton's husband were delegates—the two women discussed the idea of a women's rights convention. Later in Seneca Falls, where Stanton resided, they solidified plans and on July 19, 1848, the two-day Women's Rights Convention was held, with 300 people in attendance. Orator, statesman and former slave, Frederick Douglass was among the 32 male attendees who signed the Declaration of Sentiments, the founders' manifesto that stated that "all men and women are created equal."

Key Figures

★★★★★★★

Lucretia Mott	(1793-1880)
Elizabeth Cady Stanton	(1815-1902)
Susan B. Anthony	(1820-1906)

Beginning in 1852, Susan B. Anthony, the daughter of a Quaker abolitionist, worked in close collaboration with her friend Elizabeth Cady Stanton on women's rights. In particular, Anthony's lecture tours and attempts to vote were highly publicized.

The Women's Rights National Historical Park encompasses several diverse locations important to the history of the women's rights movement. At its heart is the visitor center, where exhibits explore themes of womanhood and address contemporary issues. Next door, Declaration Park contains the remains of Wesleyan Chapel, where the 1848 convention took place. Other park sites include Elizabeth Cady Stanton's house. Though not part of the park, the National Women's Hall of Fame, at 76 Fall Street, honors women from all walks of life, adding new inductees each year.

Address: 136 Fall Street

Phone: 315-568-2991

www.nps.gov/wori

United Nations of Commerce
World Trade Center Site

One of Many Memorials Commemorating September 11, 2001 — © Martha Cooper

New York, New York

For nearly 30 years, the twin 110-story towers of the World Trade Center dominated lower Manhattan's skyline. Each skyscraper rose to 1,350 feet, making them the second-tallest buildings in the U.S. after Sears Tower in Chicago. Dubbed the "United Nations of Commerce," the World Trade Center became the central market of global trade, hosting a concentration of all international business services and some 50,000 workers within its seven-building complex. On the morning of September 11, 2001, two hijacked commercial airliners were deliberately flown into the twin towers. Within an hour and a half, both towers collapsed, effectively destroying the entire complex. In the aftermath of evacuation, rescue and cleanup efforts, an estimated 2,800 people were reported dead or missing, including 70 law-enforcement officers and over 300 firefighters killed in the line of duty. For months, search and clearing operations continued around the clock, drawing skilled volunteer workers from around the country.

Defining Moments: 1972

Two years after David Rockefeller, head of Chase Manhattan Bank, proposed the idea of a trade center in 1960, legislation was passed authorizing the Port of New York Authority to realize the project. Architects Minoru Yamasaki & Associates and Emery Roth & Sons designed the complex, and construction began in 1966. The south tower was completed in 1972, the north tower in 1973.

The attack on the World Trade Center in 2001 was not the first. On February 26, 1993, a terrorist bomb rocked one of the towers, killing six and injuring more than 1,000 persons.

Ground Zero

The recovery site includes the 16 acres of the demolished complex, much of the World Financial Center to the west, Church Street and adjacent side streets to the east, and affected blocks to the north and south. Impromptu memorials of flowers, photos, condolence notes and stuffed animals have sprung up along the site's perimeter, as New Yorkers and visitors from around the world have come to witness the extent of destruction and remember those who died.

On July 4, 2004, the cornerstone was laid for Freedom Tower, a 1,776-foot tall building (408 feet taller than the World Trade Center towers) devoted to retail and office space. Designed by Skidmore, Owings & Merrill and Studio Daniel Liebeskind, the glass-encased tower is one of several new projects slated to transform the site.

Unconventional Construction

The conventional skyscraper is generally built with a maze of interior columns. These towers, however, more resembled a steel tube than a steel cage. The architects used a new structural design in which the exterior walls would bear most of the load, maximizing open, column-free floor space. Closely spaced steel columns formed the outer walls. The aluminum-clad columns were joined by spandrel beams girdling the towers at every floor. The tight alternation of the columns and recessed floor-to-ceiling tinted windows gave the towers their trademark windowless look.

Address: Bounded by Church, Liberty, West and Barclay Streets, Lower Manhattan

Phone: 212-962-2300

www.renewnyc.com

Wright Brothers Memorial — © National Park Service

Kill Devil Hills, North Carolina

A granite boulder atop the dunes in the town of Kill Devil Hills on North Carolina's Outer Banks marks the spot where, in 1903, Wilbur and Orville Wright made the first sustained powered flight. Now known as the Wright Brothers National Memorial, the site includes reconstructions of the airplane hangar and workshop where the Wrights put finishing touches on their Flyer. A 60-foot granite shaft commemorates their epic flight—a flight that would revolutionize mankind's modes of transportation.

"... There is some hope that, for some limited purposes at least, man will eventually be able to fly through the air."

Wilbur Wright, address to the Western Society of Engineers, September 1901.

Defining Moments: 1903

Near Kitty Hawk, off North Carolina's Atlantic coast, the brothers found that the high, soft dunes and strong prevailing winds provided an ideal combination for flight experiments. Drawing from the experiences of German aeronautical engineer Otto Lilienthal and other flight pioneers, they developed a glider controlled by "wing warping"—changing the shapes of the wing tips to deflect air.

After many failed attempts, the Wrights built their own wind tunnel so they could correct problems of lift. The aircraft they developed in 1902 had a longer wingspan than their earlier designs and vertical tails to control right and left movement.

Their 1903 Flyer was a larger version of the 1902 model, equipped with a 12-horsepower engine that drove two pusher propellers. On the morning of December 17, 1903, Orville Wright climbed aboard the Flyer and launched the 605-pound machine into the air. The longest of their four flights that day was 852 feet in 59 seconds.

Although there was little publicity about the brothers' breakthrough until 1905, the Wrights patented their work and went on to build an airplane factory in Dayton, Ohio. Today Wilbur and Orville's 1903 Flyer is on display at the National Air and Space Museum in Washington, D.C.

The Years Before Kitty Hawk

Born to Bishop Milton Wright and his wife, Susan, Wilbur (1867–1912) and Orville (1871–1948) Wright were the third and fourth of five children. Wilbur was born in Milville, Indiana; Orville was born in Dayton, Ohio, where the family later moved. A toy helicopter given as a present to young Wilbur and Orville in 1878 sparked a passion for flight that remained with the boys throughout their lives.

In 1892 dreamy Wilbur and outgoing Orville opened a bicycle shop in Dayton, Ohio. The Wright Cycle Company prospered, but the brothers remained unfulfilled. Their

Courtesy National Air and Space Museum

energies finally became focused on flight in 1896, the year they learned of the death of German glider pilot Otto Lilienthal in a flying accident, and of Samuel Langley's success flying a model plane over the Potomac River. Confident that they could improve on the work that had already been done in this field, the Wright brothers set out in 1900 to build an airplane.

Address: Milepost 8, off US-158

Phone: 252-441-7430

www.nps.gov/wrbr

Victory for Independence
Yorktown National Battlefield

Yorktown National Battlefield— © Virginia Tourism Corporation

Yorktown, Virginia

Yorktown National Battlefield preserves the site of the last major battle of the American Revolution. The victory here in 1781 of General George Washington's army of American and French soldiers over the forces of British general Lord Cornwallis freed the 13 colonies forever of English control and prepared the way for the creation of an independent nation. The battlefield is part of Colonial National Historical Park, which encompasses 5,000 acres on the bluffs above the York River. Moore House, where the terms of surrender were discussed, and Yorktown National Cemetery, where Union soldiers killed in the Civil War are buried, are part of the park.

Defining Moments: 1781

By mid-1781 the Americans and the British had been at war for nearly six years. From the war's inception, naval power had been a crucial determinant of the conflict's course; for Britain, it was vital to the success of her small ground forces. Britain's enemy France—and young Marquis de Lafayette in particular—had been aiding the colonists in their struggle. The arrival of French troops in 1780 and French naval support a year later greatly strengthened the colonists' position.

In September 1781, the British fleet reached Yorktown. The next day, 24 French ships entered Chesapeake Bay. In the ensuing engagement, the French navy chased out the British ships and established a blockade in the bay, hemming in Cornwallis and his men at Yorktown. To the north, Lafayette's troops blocked any escape by land. When Washington appeared with 7,000 allied French and American troops, the Continental forces in Virginia numbered 17,600—more than double the size of Cornwallis' army.

"I have the mortification to inform your Excellency that I have been forced to...surrender the troops under my command."

Dispatch from Lord Cornwallis, October, 1781

By mid-October, the allied forces had captured all 10 British redoubts (small enclosed forts) that encircled Yorktown, and the British were desperate. Faced with a hopeless situation, Cornwallis surrendered his entire army to Washington on October 19. The 1781 Siege of Yorktown dashed any remaining hopes Britain had of victory over the colonists. In September 1783, Britain signed the Treaty of Paris, which recognized the independence of all 13 American colonies.

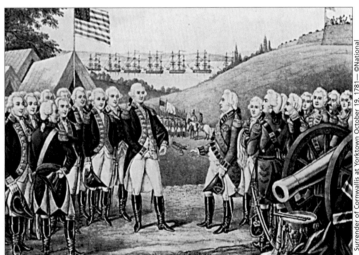

Surrender of Cornwallis at Yorktown October 19, 1781— ©National Archives and Records Administration

Address: East end of the Colonial Parkway

Phone: 757-898-2410

www.nps.gov/yonb

Maps ■ Road Atlases ■ Travel Guides

Michelin Road Atlases:
Designed for the way you drive

2005 North America Road Atlas
North America Midsize Road Atlas
Regional Road Atlases

Road Atlas +
Travel Guide Series:
More than an Atlas, more than a Guide

California	Pacific Coast
Florida	Pacific Northwest
Great Lakes	Québec
Gulf Coast	Southeast USA
Mid-Atlantic USA	Southwest USA
New England	Texas
Northeast Corridor	Western Canada

The Must Sees:
Maximize the fun and minimize the guesswork of travel

Boston and Cape Cod	Los Angeles	San Francisco
The Caribbean	Montreal	SC Coast
Chicago	New Orleans	Toronto
Hawaiian Islands	New York City	Vancouver
Las Vegas	Orlando	Washington, DC
London	Paris	

TO ORDER

UNITED STATES
Online: www.michelin-us.com
Phone: 1-888-610-5122
Michelin Travel Publications
One Parkway South
Greenville, SC 29615

CANADA
1-800-361-8236, Fax 1-800-361-6937
Michelin Travel Publication
2540, Boul. Daniel-Johnson, Suite 510
Laval, Québec, H7T 2T9

Custom Products
**Looking for unique promotional tools for
your business or organization**
Michelin offers a wide variety of customization options that are sure t
make great impact at an affordable cost. For more details, please contact u